HOW TO MAKE MONEY
Writing Short Articles
And Fillers

HOW TO MAKE MONEY
Writing Short Articles
And Fillers

by

Marjorie M. Hinds

author of

HOW TO WRITE FOR THE JUVENILE MARKET

A World of Books That Fill a Need

Frederick Fell, Inc.   New York

To the memory of

Marion

whose own talent and creative ability

furnished me the incentive to achieve.

CONTENTS

HOW TO MAKE MONEY
Writing Short Articles
And Fillers

CHAPTER ONE

Surveying the Field

Without doubt, writing fillers and articles is the most promising of all branches of free-lance writing. It is as creative as fiction and equally rewarding. For the beginning writer, it is an especially good field. Often those who are unable to sell fiction can still be successful in article writing because it does not require the complicated plotting technique that is inclined to bog down the amateur.

Since you are interested in learning how to write fillers and articles, it is well that you familiarize yourself with the field and its demands upon you if you would see your work published. This chapter presents a rather complete survey of what the field itself has to offer.

Just why is the filler and article field so attractive? It has several distinct advantages.

The filler provides one of the surest means of *breaking into print*. Because it is unlimited in its market, in its subject matter, and in its scope of treatment, there is for the amateur little or no competition with already established authors. We are accustomed to seeing big-name writers in our nationally-circulated magazines and readily agree that their skillful technique has put them there. Yet the editors of those same magazines are encouraging *new* writers to submit short copy to them. In other words, the door is already open. You have but to learn how to approach it and step inside.

The market is a *wide* one. Over 5,000 periodicals of all classes in circulation today as well as over 1,800 daily newspapers use fillers. Every editor is compelled to have on hand a substantial stock of these short pieces ready for use at a moment's notice as the paper or magazine is in printing process. Therefore the market for short items is limitless.

The *variety of subjects* for fillers is *limitless,* as well. In no other field of writing can a beginner launch so easily upon topics of his own liking. Sports, business, music, jokes, news, recipes, odd facts, art, homemaking, children, history, nature, editorials, inspirational items— all these and many more are included in the vast field of short-item writing. Never is the writer confined to any subject out of his own line of interest. And naturally what we like to do we are more likely to excel in.

Most short items can be written during *spare time*. For one who has other interests or occupation, fillers make an ideal outlet for that creative urge and still consume a minimum of his time. Style is not specifically important, and little rewriting is required in certain kinds.

Writing short items provides opportunity for an *early start at earning*. This does not mean that just anyone can write nor that sloppy-Joe writing is ever permissible. But since every filler, no matter how short, requires essentially the same skillful technique as a longer piece, once a person gets the "hang" of it so that he can produce a little every day, he has helped to bring in a substantial weekly income for himself. In other words, fillers provide basic training in a profitable way.

One nationally-circulated magazine pays $5 each for 100- to 300-word fillers and uses 20 a month. Two others, paying $1 to $5 for very short paragraphs, use literally dozens each month. In one specialized field alone there are over 1,500 editors looking for short copy. One magazine pays $10 for every joke printed; another, $100 for the best letter of the month; needless to remind you that *Reader's Digest* pays $25 for each quotation in one of its departments and $100 for each anecdote used in "Life in These United States."

In no other field is there such an *opportunity to duplicate checks* for the same idea. Many a successful writer of short items can sell his idea twenty-five times, treating it in just a little different manner when submitting to various editors. Later on you will see how this can be done effectively, saving time and research, and at the same time bringing in many, many more checks.

And while we are discussing the many advantages filler and article writing offers, let us not forget that many big-name writers of our day now frankly confess that it was their *short copy* production that kept them in food until they became established. Sinclair Lewis, the first American to win the Nobel Prize for literature, wrote novels feverishly and unsuccessfully until he made the discovery of turning out short items. Incidentally, his first sale was a single joke to *Judge*. Booth Tarkington began his career by writing household items. Joseph Hergesheimer, after years of struggle, had his first manuscript accepted by *Good Housekeeping*. It was a stuffed cabbage recipe published in his wife's name! Jack London, Mary Roberts Rinehart, and many others got their start by writing fillers simply because they realized how quickly they could turn their efforts into cash.

Having discussed, then, the place and merits of filler writing as a beginner's venture, let's make sure we understand just what a filler is and what purpose it serves. It is any short piece of writing an editor uses between longer articles or stories. It can range from twenty-five to a few hundred words. It can even be a quatrain or a couplet in a poetry magazine. It is very often a cartoon or comic strip, or perhaps a quiz or a game. In a word, it is any little device an editor uses to lend variety to his needs. He does not in desperation turn to just any short item he might glean from an almanac or dead pile of papers at his elbow; he actually plans positions for them. And those fillers must carry reader appeal as well.

For our study here we shall use the word *filler* as it applies only to *very short* pieces. *Articles,* then, range for the most part from 600 to 5,000 words. We shall try to show what type of writing has the greatest appeal to the reading public as well as to show you just how to write and sell acceptable work.

The field of filler writing is a very flexible one. If an idea is not worth developing into a full-length piece, it can be adapted to a short; if the subject matter warrants it both as to importance and appeal, a longer piece. And at no time has the 600 to 1,000 word article been so popular as at present.

To succeed in this type of writing you will find that a few definite qualities are essential. No matter how good a teacher is, there is no one who can teach you everything about how to write. Some of it must come from within—a love of writing and a genuine desire to learn the right approach. It is safe to say that those who can be developed into writers *do* experience a decided urge to write and are eager, with the natural ability that they have, to develop it. But remember that writing is a business like any other. Believe in yourself and in your ability. It is as essential to have courage as it is to have talent. Tackle the job with enthusiasm, and above all, remember that instruction is like medicine, of no value unless you follow directions.

It is only reasonable to assume that upon engaging in *any* kind of work, a person should expect to learn certain "keys" to the craft. Writing is not without its "keys," too, "keys" that every writer should employ. The first is that of *reading*. The average person is guilty of minimizing its importance as a background to writing. His impatience and urge to "get started" can often spell defeat for him. But an editor is not to be fooled. Like a teacher, he can detect the difference between the writing of a student who reads and that of the nonreaders. We are not implying that one should steal someone else's material nor do we condone pure imitation of something already in print. It does follow, however, that the more we've been nourished in our own reading, the more health and vigor will be reflected in our own writing efforts.

Almost everyone uses in his writing the kind of English he is ordinarily exposed to. So the way you write depends largely on what you read. If you want to write well, you must read good material. Some of the qualities found there are bound to "rub off."

How can you tell good writing when you see it? It is quite simple. The good writer knows the tricks of his trade and uses them to make us think and feel the way he wants us to; the poor writer, not understanding his business, never really touches our minds or hearts.

The term "good writing" is not used here to denote

something dull or antiquated or something that has been declared a classic in years gone by. We mean writing that is rewarding, writing that has meat in it, writing that is enjoyable to read. Writing that really comes alive because the author has learned to fuse his feelings with those of his reader.

Now since you are launching upon filler and article writing for at least a part-time enterprise, you should "saturate" yourself with published fillers and articles every opportunity you get. Choose a variety of magazines and study several issues of each. Don't read them simply for amusement, information, and the like. Study the style, the length, the terseness of the author. Subconsciously you will be absorbing the very elements that *you* will be needing if *you* are to succeed.

The second "key" necessary for a writer is a *time schedule*. If your aim is a serious one and you are determined to become a writer, it is imperative from the very beginning that you assign yourself a specific hour each day and stick to it. The hour you give yourself should not be spent looking around for ideas; it should not be spent *geting ready* to write. Resist all the tempting distractions that arise and use that time in actual creative work.

The specific length of time for which you can comfortably write is something you will have to work out for yourself. It is different for every writer. A little experimentation will reveal what your average wordage output is likely to be and about how much time it will take you to set down that many words. If you can arrange for more than an hour a day, all the better, but be faithful to it. Many of our most popular writers tell us that at an early stage of their writing they set for themselves a goal of no fewer than 500 words a day. They like to think of it as a wordage schedule rather than a time schedule. Whichever you choose, the main idea is to stick with it!

May we inject a thought here while we are discussing working habits? The question often arises, "Should one use a typewriter or can he write with a pencil?" Here again, experimentation will reveal the best method for you. Probably most people write their first work in pencil and it would seem natural that they do so. Some always write with a pencil—even full book length— and then type the manuscript when finished. But you will find with experience that you can really cultivate the habit of "thinking" on the typewriter. It will be hard at first; the blank paper will frighten you. Especially valuable is this practice, though, for the writer of fillers. After all, the profit for short items is small at best, and if you write and write and then rewrite, you consume so much time that you have no financial reward for the effort expended.

The third "key" is *persistence*. Nobody is born with writing technique; it is something you have to learn. And you learn by daily practice with words the same as a musician learns his instrument by daily practice with notes. To make money out of writing you somehow have to learn to turn out good, clean, well-written copy *fast*.

Let's assume that you have finished what you think is a splendid little filler of about 500 words. It is *simple* (and that's one of the fundamentals of good style in any kind of writing); you have made it as *concise* as you know how without leaving out important details;

you have made yourself *clear* in the point you were trying to make. You have read it and re-read it. It satisfies
you. You mail it to a prospective buyer.

Now don't wait! Here is the beginner's pitfall. The
minute you have mailed an article (or in the case of
very short fillers we usually mail about three), forget
it. Take no vacations between writing jobs. With experience you will find that before you finish one piece,
ideas for another will be taking shape in your mind, anyhow, so as soon as you abandon one filler, adopt another.

If that first one comes back from one market, there
are often a number of others that might take it without
further slanting. Perhaps you'll want to re-type it but
that will not take long. Study the market possibilities
and get it off to another editor the same day. Continuous
output is a "must" if you are going to realize any financial
gain. It's a proverbial truth that "an article not in the
mail has no chance of selling." Some writers keep as many
as one hundred fillers out at one time. They have come
to see, too, that it is extremely important for material
to be kept moving. By the law of averages, you can
readily see that their chances of checks are far better,
too. Many who have ability are still not successful writers
because they lack *persistence*.

The fourth "key" to the writing craft is the indispensable notebook. We say *"indispensable"* because the
experienced writer has already learned that it has become
a *habit* with him. And you in your early attempts to
gather subject material will soon see how vitally important it is to carry with you wherever you go a small
one for jottings and to have a larger one at home. Impressions, novelties, even unique ideas are soon "lost"
if they are not recorded. As time goes by, if you're really

serious about the whole thing, you will discover that the notebook is the writer's best friend.

The last "key" can unlock hundreds of possibilities for the writer of fillers and articles. It is as important as the road map to the tourist or the product to the salesman. It is your *clipping file*. No great expense need be involved; rather, the important thing is a system of reference material planned to serve you effectively as a backlog for article writing. Two sets of manila folders or envelopes should be arranged alphabetically for two purposes: (1) to hold specimens of the various *types* of fillers and ideas that you come across in your reading and (2) *features* of writing skill that appeal to you and which you feel can serve as specimens for further study (titles, good beginnings, dialogue, effective endings, etc.).

Learn to "clip" and file while the ideas are fresh in your mind. Red ink the feature of the published article that caused you to clip it for ready reference.

CHAPTER TWO

Where to Get Ideas

In any writers' magazine that you may have subscribed to or in any textbook you have read on writing technique, you have noticed, I am sure, this familiar sentence: *Ideas are everywhere.* But no matter how familiar, the importance of such a statement should not be minimized. The tendency too often is to ignore the very "jewels" under our feet because we regard them as commonplace. And, strangely enough, it's the commonplace things in life, presented in a style that is attractive to the general public's taste, that *have* appeal. Yes, everything about us is—or should be—grist to a writer's mill.

Be sure, though, from the very start to form the notebook habit (referred to in Chapter One) of recording those "jewels." Often an idea will pop into your mind and you'll recognize it as especially good filler material, only to return later and discover that the details associated with it have grown cold. You can't recall them. The original spark is missing. If only you had jotted down three sentences on a scrap of paper!

Everyday experiences can furnish us with limitless possibilities in the field of filler and article writing. Let's examine some of our resources.

I. PERSONAL OBSERVATION

Too many of us would have to agree with the poet: "Little we see in Nature that is ours." We must train ourselves to *see* what we look at. Personal observation that is alert and meaningful supplies many writers with fifty per cent of their ideas. It can serve *you* equally as generous a turn if you, too, will form the habit of analyzing what you see and hear about you, and then cull out details most pertinent to the subject.

Suppose, for example, you've heard of a recent fundraising stunt, or a public auction that is different, a St. Valentine's Day party, a new use for old photograph albums, the new toy devised by a neighbor. All these and hundreds more can serve as potential check-cashers. Let me illustrate.

My father, a pharmacist, had had throughout his many years in business some rare over-the-counter experiences. His ability to relate vividly such incidents, coupled with an exceptionally keen sense of humor, made it possible for me to "catch in my lap" many gems for fillers. The first sale I ever made, in fact, was the result of a child customer's answer to him. I never added or subtracted one word from the original statement! Since then I have on occasion asked friends who are in business to relate human-interest experiences and thereby have capitalized on many. Dentists, hardware dealers, bankers, grocery clerks, ministers can often furnish us with excellent material for article development.

The simplest kind of short item to write is one that deals with an unusual place or object. Perhaps there's a familiar landmark in your area that has an interesting history. It may be worth money to you instead of just a glance. Perhaps among your acquaintances is a person with an unusual but fascinating hobby. That information might well be turned into a salable article. Children at play, or even in serious mood, often say priceless things. With a "listening" ear you can pick up fillers from them. Listen constantly and consciously. Is your interest gardening, mechanics, nature study, art, candy-making, or photography? They're at your service. And if you can't "see" a good filler at home, you won't see it elsewhere.

Even a vacation can serve as an opportunity to gather material for articles. Visiting a scenic spot on the coast of Maine several years ago, I became very much interested in Mount Desert Rock Lighthouse. I was told it was the most exposed light station on the Atlantic coast and that during severe gales the sea breaks entirely over the rock. Reports have it that a rock of seventy-five tons has been moved sixty feet during a storm. I suddenly realized that here was the nucleus for an informational filler. I thought of those in responsible positions, giving warnings, and of the life of keepers' families. Jotting down all the facts gleaned there served as a preface to an eight-hundred-word article that I developed later.

These suggestions are, of course, only a few of the many possibilities for turning simple, everyday things into published fillers. The amount of encouragement you'll get from your first little checks can never be measured in dollars and cents. But most people agree that they get more enjoyment by writing and seeing themselves published than by doing any other kind of work.

II. THE NEWSPAPER

One of the best sources for vital filler and article topics is the newspaper. Whether one is interested in business and trade journal writing, or biography, or general informative pieces, ideas for such articles abound in daily issues. It is not a question of copying a news item, which would be silly and unethical. It is a matter of learning how to read a newspaper and how to cull the nuggets of human interest that would be suitable for article development. Remember that you are culling only *facts*, and facts belong to everybody, not by copyright. The writing and handling of the material must be *yours*.

Frankly, after one has adopted the "newspaper habit," he may find himself so completely overcome with the vast number of ideas and how best to use them that the whole process seems to bottleneck for him. You may find, in that case, that it's best to settle on a certain number of items—perhaps three or four a day—that you are most interested in. And make sure you steer away from headline stories. The *real* nuggets are in those little two and three paragraph items often tucked away inside the paper.

As you scan for subjects, be sure to clip the possibilities you find and paste them in a notebook. List the name of the newspaper and the date. Time may pass before you develop some of the items, but they will furnish you a backlog of material. Most of the time you'll have to do some research.

It is well, however, in case the item deals with a person's achievement, record, or the like, to contact him by letter at once, explaining that you are interested in learning more and what you intend to do with the information when you get it. Delay in securing the data, even though you delay in writing it up, can dull your enthusiasm as well as affect the other person's response to your request. In preparing a questionnaire for such a purpose, space your questions on the page so that the subject can answer directly beneath; he'll know then how much information you want on each question. At the bottom, give him a little more freedom of expression by asking such questions as: "What was your most enjoyable experience? Your greatest surprise? Your funniest experience?" And most important, ask him to relate one or two good anecdotes.

There's a certain sense of security for the writer as he gleans the newspaper for ideas. Since the items already represent what the public is interested in (or they wouldn't be printed), the writer is assured before he starts that the finished product will have reader appeal. Hundreds of writers scan the dailies as though they were looking for gold. They cull, they write, they sell. At the same time, though, hundreds of *other* writers all over the country are reading those same dispatches reported by Associated Press and United Press. Competition, you can see at a glance, is terrific.

In my opinion, a more practical approach to newspaper help, at least for the beginner, is the *weekly* paper. Based on my own sales experience, I have found that collecting checks is far easier if one sticks to clipping so-called *local incidents*. "But," you say, "I have none. I always read a daily." Well, somewhere near you there's bound to be a county or small-town weekly that will supply you with just the kind of material you need.

Let me illustrate how this "culling" process works

by tracing step by step as clearly as I can one of my own newspaper experiences.

I picked up a small-town weekly one morning with the express purpose of spotting subjects. I had not long to wait. At the extreme right were these headlines: LOCAL BOY NAMED STAR FARMER. The subheading read: "Hamlin Township Young Man Given Honor at National Gathering." Accompanying the news item were four pictures, one of the lad himself and three others featuring him at work on his farm. Upon reading further, I discovered that he was the first boy ever to be selected from this particular region by the national organization Future Farmers. I clipped the item immediately and before the day was over I had prepared an easy-to-answer questionnaire to send to him, at the same time explaining that I was interested in securing further data so that I might write a 1,000-word article for one of the many farm journals. The boy was unusually cooperative and soon I had such facts as these returned to me: (1) He had graduated with top honors from high school; (2) was prominent in school activities; (3) had made $300 in his elementary grades from a farm project; (4) by the time he entered senior high school he owned 600 chickens, 3 dairy calves, and considerable crops of oats and corn and (5) by graduation time he owned 31 head of cattle, 300 chickens, 36 acres of hay, 31 acres of small grain, and a net profit of $3,108. I knew at once here was material I could use and that the article would be written and sold.

But to get back to my paper. On that same page of the weekly I noticed a picture of the Galusha A. Grow homestead which had recently been dedicated as an historic shrine to the man who a century ago had introduced the Homestead Act into the records of our country.

Below it was a picture of a monument erected on a village green some twenty miles away, this, too, in honor of the pioneer "expansionist." Something clicked. Why wouldn't this be a good subject for another 1,000-worder? Probably a juvenile story paper for boys would be the best outlet. It seemed an incredibly short time before these words came out of my typewriter:

> On a small village green in Northeastern Pennsylvania stands a simple stone monument, erected to a man whose signature on an important document nearly a century ago created the greatest stir for expansion our country has ever known.
>
> What a sight you might have witnessed had you been camped along the Mississippi River that April day when the rush began! People in wagons, in carriages, on horseback, and on foot—all wildly excited—pushed and shoved each other feverishly. Up and down the border the guards walked, keeping the anxious people back. As the hour of twelve approached, the strain neared the breaking point.
>
> Then an officer rode to the highest point of ground in the area. At exactly noon he blew a blast on the bugle, at the same time dropping a flag.
>
> Like bullets from guns the people shot over the line and were off on the great race for homes. Yes, America's last frontier was about to be settled. And all because a man like Galusha A. Grow had the vision of an America we know today.
>
> Etc., etc.

I looked on through the newspaper. A page three heading caught my fancy. It concerned a county woman

who, here in the month of June, was literally stuffing her
house with toys for Christmas. I hastened to clip, for it
had been several weeks since I had written a piece for
a hobby magazine.

I found Mrs. Edstrom equally cooperative in giving
me information needed for a short article. With a work
room that looked like a miniature zoo and tables full of
cutouts and half-finished toys, she explained enthusiasti-
cally how she came to get started in this business, what
materials were needed, length of time the average toy
consumed, kinds of patterns used, and the various outlets
she had for her merchandise. She had kept an accurate
account of all expenditures since her workshop days began. The average toy cost her 21c and she was selling
each for one dollar. Even large department stores had
recently become interested in stocking them and she
was considering at the moment taking on help and ex-
panding the business.

There are many magazines that are interested in
such facts, especially for women readers, so it came with
no surprise that an eight-hundred-word article accompanied by an eight by ten gloss print should interest an
editor.

I looked no further. Three a week from that *one*
source was all that I could handle with other assign-
ments, and I much prefer to write soon after the idea
strikes me than after I have allowed it to grow cold. Besides, there lay the daily paper.

Another example of what a mere news item can
develop into is shown by an incident that took place
several years ago. The fact was related in a daily paper
that a letter written by Jenny Lind to her aunt in Sweden
had just been added to the collection of Lindiana at the

American Swedish Historical Museum in South Philadelphia. There was particular emphasis on the fact that the letter had been written on an Easter morning to reveal that love had come to the famous singer and given her what she desired far more than fortune and fame.

Any writer could use this little news item as a springboard if his eyes were alert to the human interest it contained. This is the way the 1,000-word piece, "The Diva's Love Letter," appeared later. (Printed here with permission of *Philadelphia Inquirer.*)

The Diva's Love Letter

The sun of Easter Sunday flooded the Massachusetts countryside with golden light, but April winds were chill and snow covered Northhampton gardens in the year of 1852. But it was warm and pleasant inside a white cottage where a bride sat at a little desk ecstatically pouring the story of her happiness into a letter.

She was not a young girl venturing outside her home for the first time on a timid honeymoon. She was 32 (considered almost too old for marriage in those days) and she knew and was known in every capital in Europe, every city in the United States.

In Munich, Vienna, Budapest, London, multitudes had adored and cheered her. In Berlin, students had unharnessed the horses from her carriage and struggled for the honor of drawing it through the streets. When she had come to this country, some 30,000 persons were waiting to welcome her at the dock and New York City celebrated for twenty-four hours.

The great composer, Mendelssohn, had been in love with her. Twice she had been engaged, once to a famed opera singer, later to a dashing young army captain. But only now, long after she had despaired of finding simple, peaceful happiness, had love come to her and given her what she desired far more than fortune or fame. And on this Easter Sunday, she was putting the wonder of it into a letter home.

Today that letter—artless, almost naïve, hinting at the pious preoccupations which characterized the writer—is a recent addition to the collection of Lindiana at the American Swedish Historical Museum in South Philadelphia. For it was written by Jenny Lind, the famous singer, to her aunt in Ostersund, Sweden.

Near the glass case which holds the letter is an old daguerreotype of the "Swedish Nightingale" and the husband, nine years her junior, she so loved. He was Otto Goldschmidt, the serious young German pianist whom P. T. Barnum rounded up to be her accompanist when the great showman brought her across for her triumphal tour of this country. Taken in Boston soon after the wedding in February, 1852, the picture shows Otto's arm around his bride and the two holding hands as would any rapturous young couple.

News of Jenny's marriage had already been carried by the public prints to her native land— astonishing news to many who questioned her choice of a virtually unknown and comparatively humble pianist for a husband.

But on that Easter Sunday in the honeymoon

cottage she offered the other side of the picture, the side the public never saw, to Mrs. Eva Christina Pehrman, the sister of her dead mother:

"*My dearly beloved Aunt! I can no longer wait to write to you, my dear aunt, of the important news which probably has already reached your ears, namely this, that I was married two months ago. I know that my aunt's loving heart takes a great interest in my well-being, and that you will be glad to know that in my husband I have found all the earthly support that I have needed for such a long time and for which I secretly have asked God.*

"*I have found the most noble and beautiful character and heart, together with the clearest and deepest intelligence. We are born for each other. This I dare to say, because even our thoughts are in agreement, also our hearts; and the music, this beautiful, pure gift from above, lives richly in us both; and Music and Religion were the two most important attributes necessary to my happiness in the married life.*

"*My husband is a great pianist and thoroughly educated in every way. Yes, my dear aunt, God has given me in my beloved husband all the wonderful joy which I never found before through my parents or brothers and sisters. And it would be my fault if I did not understand how to retain my happiness, because my husband, although younger than myself, is entirely reliable and incapable of acting otherwise than God expects a man to act toward his wife.*"

Dr. Marshall W. S. Swan, curator of the American Swedish Historical Museum, considers the letter one of the outstanding treasures of the Lind collection. It was the gift of Ormond Rambo, Jr., Philadelphia investment broker and president of the board of governors of the Museum, who obtained it when the library of Mrs. Mary Sefton Thomas Lux was auctioned in New York recently. Mr. Rambo is a direct descendant of Peter Gunnarsson Rambo, one of the first magistrates in the colony of Pennsylvania and one of the earliest Swedish colonists to settle in the United States in the seventeenth century.

Contrary to plans, Jenny Lind did not live in Germany after her return to Europe with her husband. Instead they went first to London, where Otto had been elected leader of the celebrated Bach Choir, then found a permanent home in surburban Malvern. And despite raised eyebrows and headshakes, the marriage turned out as supremely successful. Jenny felt she had touched the heights of happiness when her two sons and daughter were born.

Without regret the "Swedish Nightingale" stilled her voice not many years after her marriage. A gentle, shy girl whose blue eyes always gazed out in fright over throngs gathered to hear her sing, her entire career was harassed by anxiety. She doubted her own ability, questioned her right to aspire to fame, was feverishly eager to be finished with theatrical life.

Yet she insisted upon making her own decision to leave it. This insistence was responsible for her broken engagement to opera singer Julius Guenther, later to Captain Claudius Harris, of Her Majesty's

Indian Service. Both men made it plain that they wished no famous career woman for a wife.

But after she became Mrs. Goldschmidt, Jenny gave a farewell concert for American audiences at Castle Garden in May, 1852; then, in England, practically limited her appearance to singing in oratorios and massed choirs under the baton of her husband. Her golden voice was last heard at a concert for charity in London four years before her death in 1887.

So, you see, a tiny news item from a daily paper turned into a 1,000-word article with just a little research and imagination. In summary, our advice to the writer of fillers and articles? Become a newspaper "clipper."

III. MAGAZINES, BOOKS, AND PAMPHLETS

First, let me repeat a warning. Using magazines as a source for fillers does *not* mean taking a filler from one, rewriting it, and submitting it to another. But anyone who forms the habit of reading and studying current magazines will profit in two ways: (1) He will find the best examples of what editors today *want,* and (2) he will find that the articles themselves will stimulate ideas for other articles.

For instance, as I was reading a general household magazine one day, I came across an article entitled "What's in a Name?" I merely scanned the pages long enough to see that the author, using the well-known words of Shakespeare for his title, was presenting some little sidelights on the meanings of many of our common names. I didn't need to read the article; the title was as far as I cared to go. In a few moments I had set myself to working out a *name puzzle*. It was short, fun to do, and sold immediately to a juvenile story paper as a filler.

I recall, too, picking up a magazine one time—I believe it was *Ladies' Home Journal*—and noticing on one of its pages a picture of Flanders Fields, with the rows upon rows of nameless graves. Below was this caption:

> His country asked his life;
> His life he gave!
>
> Lunt

As I continued to study the picture, my thoughts turned to a poem born out of that same war, "I Have a Rendezvous With Death." I thought of young Alan Seegar whose life had been snuffed out at an early age because he had heard the call of his country. Then I remembered that the poem had been found on the back of a soiled envelope in the pocket of his uniform. The poet lay dead on the battlefield when the discovery was made. Right then I reached for my scratch pad and wrote "Seegar—Rendezvous." See how easy it was for a picture to suggest an article?

One hint I'd like to pass on to you that I have found invaluable. Reading magazines that are entirely apart from the field of our interest can open up and stir up for us an endless amount of "new" ideas for writing. For example, if you normally read every travel magazine that comes your way, you will do well to turn to a scientific type. It may call upon your imagination somewhat but at least it will keep you from getting into a rut by reading only in your favorite fields.

Idea experiences can often come from reading *books* as well. It is not unlikely that many of our big-name writers get ideas from one another. Books of biography furnish data for anniversary articles. Travel books offer countless possibilities for informative pieces. Even history books, with their already familiar facts, can open new avenues to us if we use new approaches and treatment to the facts, searching out the unusual or romantic side of those events.

Neither do we realize what a store of information is ours in *pamphlets* that cost us nothing. There are literally thousands of them available for the asking. A gold mine, truly, to the writer who is handicapped by the insufficient resources of a small-town library or with no library at all.

For instance, suppose you wished to write a short article on Mt. McKinley. An abundant supply of material will be furnished free by the National Park Service, Dept. of Interior, Chicago, Illinois.

The Pan American Coffee Bureau can supply literature on coffee facts and fancies that would take very little rewriting on the part of anyone to develop an interesting little filler.

U. S. Rubber Company makes "The Romance of Rubber" available to any who request it.

If you should be interested, for example, in ancient and modern silver, write the Towle Manufacturing Company, Newburyport, Massachusetts, for their free bulletin on the subject.

Corning Glass Works is very willing to send you "The Story of Glass" for a postage stamp.

Maybe you're interested in feeding wildlife in winter. If so, contact American Wildlife Institute, Washington, D. C., and request the bulletin by that title.

The drugstore almanacs are treasures for writers, as are mail order catalogs and the paperbound pocket books of biographies, operas, etc. Even an illustrated ad can set the wheels moving if we'll exercise our imagination.

What, then, is your responsibility as a writer? To collect and file systematically material gleaned from the writing of others that you may draw from your storehouse on quick notice.

IV. FOLLOW YOUR "BENT"!

Almost everyone has at least one thing he is vitally interested in and knows a lot about. Perhaps he has a knack for or has acquired special knowledge in one particular field. It may be a part of his profession or job, but not necessarily so. It may be a sideline or hobby. But whatever it is, capitalize on it!

Perhaps, for example, you're the best entertainer of small children in your neighborhood, or a clever sign painter, the boy or girl scout leader, an expert pie baker, an authority on antique glassware, an oil painter, one who studies birds and bird calls, a private secretary, designer and maker of your own clothes, an ingenious handyman, a golf enthusiast, or a successful cameraman. These and many more can furnish gainful knowledge on which to base short articles.

And if you are really interested in something, your writing will reflect that interest. It will come alive, have sparkle, and will be read with interest by many people.

You will enjoy writing about it; furthermore you will be paid for it.

Again, let me cite illustrations. I have been closely connected with writing for many years, having been a proofreader for publishing firms, a high school English instructor, a contributor of stories, fillers, and articles to magazines and newspapers, and an author of full-length books. In my "spare time" I have done ghost writing, revision work, and have collaborated in the writing of a series of textbooks. Still I feel that my "bent" is in the field of teaching and I assure you my notebook list of possibilities—born out of my contacts with teen-agers— will never be exhausted.

For instance, once in one of my high school classes the students were giving oral reports on the story behind certain works of literature, art, music, invention, or whatever subject interested them and which they had done research work on. Within one class period two girls reported on well-known hymns. The one chose "Nearer, My God, to Thee"; the other, "Silent Night." Fascinated by the audience response, I set to work putting those same facts into a style that would appeal to other young readers. The first resulted in "A Song is Born"; the second, "Out of the Stillness, a Song," both of which were sold to young people's magazines.

On another occasion in the classroom a lively discussion was held on the unusual facts the students had discovered in the lives of many literary figures. When I sensed the enjoyment they received from it, I realized that the idea would be no risk for other teen-agers' interest. A short filler, "Further Facts on the Famous," appeared later in a Canadian journal.

In preparing an examination one day for my American literature classes, I was prompted to give double duty to the material I had jotted down. It appeared as a puzzle filler with the title "Who's Who?" in a juvenile weekly.

The practical suggestions I pick up from others with whom I work—observing the ingenuity of the teen-agers to solve problems for themselves—yes, many a lesson the student has taught me—all these have been the nuclei for many fillers I have capitalized on. And just as many can be picked up in the experience of the housewife, the mason, or the store clerk. Try it.

THINGS TO DO

PERSONAL INVENTORY—At this point we suggest that you take a little personal inventory in relation to the material already covered. Can you answer these questions satisfactorily?

1. How do editors regard short copy from new writers?
2. What freedom does the filler field hold for the writer?
3. Why is style less important here than in fiction?
4. What is the word range of fillers?
5. Why is reading so vital to a writer?
6. What is meant by *good* writing?
7. What should be the minimum amount of time spent daily in writing practice?
8. Why should one discipline himself to "think" on the typewriter?
9. What practice should one follow in sending out fillers?

10. Why do so many writers refuse to write about things in their own backyards?
11. Why are newspaper items a sure bet for article ideas?
12. How can magazines serve as a source for filler and article ideas?
13. Why is it wise to read magazines sometimes foreign to our regular tastes?
14. What help is available to the writer handicapped by insufficient library sources?
15. What is meant by "follow your bent"?

SUGGESTIONS—1. Start a clipping file of ideas from newspapers. You may prefer nine by twelve envelopes; some like letter-size file folders. Label them as to content: "Ideas Needing Research," "Clever expressions," "Unusual Facts," etc.

2. Begin a magazine clipping file, too, to use as models.

CHAPTER THREE

How to Write Fillers
and Articles

As we pointed out earlier, the brevity and relative simplicity of fillers and short articles enable you to turn out a volume of salable pieces by writing for only a short time each day. We have also tried to emphasize the necessity of keeping a notebook and jotting down things that you hear and see, as well as clipping what appeals to you through reading.

Perhaps, for instance, one of the fellows at the office tells an amusing incident that happened at home; or the neighbor across the street relates to you one of her five year old's bright sayings. Either might prove good filler material if you know how to convert it.

Limiting fillers to a definite number of types is most difficult. But in this book we have attempted to cover some of the most popular ones, treating each separately in its appropriateness, style, and content. In every case possible we have included illustrations that have been accepted by editors. They appear not in order of length or importance, but simply in alphabetical order for your convenience in referring to them.

ANECDOTE

The anecdote is the story of a true incident in the life of an individual. It has a much wider use than the regular joke. In the first place, anecdotes are less likely to have been heard before; therefore the writer's chances for market are decidedly better. Then, too, the results in cash make them more inviting for the same amount of time and energy as expended on jokes.

Anecdotes can be very effectively used as beginnings for articles, especially if one's subject deals with a well-known individual. For instance, if you had selected Mark Twain for a personal feature article, you might be able to use something like this:

In the drowsy little town of Hannibal, Missouri, beside the mile-wide river, little Sam Clemens began to think long, long thoughts and to worry his mother with his pranks. Among other early experiments, he exposed himself to the measles and came so near dying that the family gathered tearfully around his bed to see him die, a circumstance that considerably gratified his vanity.

Years later, his mother, recalling the incident, said to him: "You gave me more uneasiness than any child I had."

"I suppose you were afraid I wouldn't live," he suggested.

She looked at him with that keen humor that her 80 years had not dulled and replied: "No, afraid that you *would*."

Or here is one that appeared in Boswell's eighteenth-century biography of Dr. Samuel Johnson.

One day Johnson and his poet friend Gold-smith were visiting Westminster Abbey together. As they gazed upon the statues of the dead, Johnson solemnly declared: "Perhaps *our* names also will be mingled with these."
Returning homeward later through the Strand, they came to Temple Bar, where, in those days, the heads of criminals were exhibited as a warning to evil-doers. Goldsmith, pointing at them, slyly repeated his friend's earlier line: "Perhaps our names also will be mingled with *these*."

Often a writer's mistake is telling so *much* before the climax that the punch of the story is lost. We must choose for ourselves the most effective way of telling the story. If the experience is actually yours, you may write it in the first person; if it's something you heard or overheard, use the third person. But regardless of which viewpoint you select, there should be a thoughtful procedure in developing the story.

Until you have had some experience with it, here is a formula that can help you get the "feel" of it. First, write out the *entire incident* for your own satisfaction. Then pick out the climax and write separately with *punch* in it. Basing your lead on story facts already written, cull out unnecessary details and condense to a sharp, pointed narration so that you have built *up to* the punch line.

For example, this was one of my early experiments based on personal observation, a simple little thing, yet

I sensed its possibilities for a write-up and sale. It worked. Notice how completely I wrote it out first, not for submission, but in order that I might keep the logical order of ideas before me.

STEP 1—As I stood waiting for a long line of cars to pass so that I could cross the street one hot July day in my home town, a workman with his lunch pail arrived at the same curb. We had barely exchanged greetings when a convertible bearing an Illinois license plate slowed up in front of us. The driver was trying to be seen above the road map into which his wife had buried her face. It was obvious that they thought they were on the wrong road. They were looking for "Blankville," which incidentally was the name of our small town. Finally the driver inquired where Blankville was. The workman in a very droll manner informed him that if he drove much farther, he'd be out of it. The driver grinned, thanked him, and drove away.

STEP 2—Select the punch line, which of course, will be a direct quotation from the workman's lips.

STEP 3—The revised anecdote
A convertible bearing an Illinois license plate slowed almost to snail pace as it passed through a tiny Pennsylvania village. The face of the driver's wife buried in a map gave evidence that neither occupant was familiar with the route.
A workman with lunch pail in hand stood waiting to cross the street. Spying him, the driver leaned

out and inquired, "Sir, could you tell me where Blankville is?"

"Heavens, man!" the workman replied. "If you drive three more rods, you'll be out of it!"

You see, not only have I cut the final copy one third of the original, but I have eliminated all unnecessary facts.

Frequently we overlook newspapers as a market for anecdotes, concentrating instead upon magazines. The pay, however, is equally inviting. A good story, carefully handled and short, can easily find its way into print. Here is one I sold to *Scranton Tribune* a number of years ago.

The small-town pharmacist looked up from his morning newspaper as the front door opened. His eyes searched the familiar face of little Edgar whose mother frequently sent him on errands. But there was something unusual about Edgar's expression this morning; a look of uncertainty was registered there. The druggist knew he had forgotten the name of the item needed.

Thinking to embarrass the little fellow, he looked over the top of his glasses fiercely and bellowed, "Well, what do you want?"

Edgar eyed him closely, then swallowed hard and asked, "Wh-wh-what's good for the head?"

Quickly the druggist snapped, "Brains!"

Whereupon the surprise came when Edgar's face brightened and he briskly asked, "Got any?"

THE BRIGHT SAYING

A close ally to the anecdote is the "bright saying" filler, but never do we find space given to this type that we do to the developed anecdote.

Who hasn't been amused by the unpredictable speeches that come "out of the mouths of babes"? Your own little tot, the kid next door, the urchin doing her mother's shopping, all of them can provide priceless material for the writer of fillers. Here are only two of the many that have been sold.

Child, seeing a soft-shelled hen's egg for the first time: "But, Daddy, why didn't he put more crust on it?"

Jimmy, four, had just been hit on the cheek by a June bug. Running to his mother, he screamed, "Oh, I was just hit by a black bug with a motor in it!"

Attune your ears to these possibilities. The world over, you'll find children. And when you do, *listen!*

EPIGRAM

An epigram is a "bright or witty thought tersely expressed and often involving an apparent contradiction." It can also appear as a short, often satirical poem, commonly ending with a witticism. Probably Alexander Pope was as well known as any English poet for his many epigrams. This, for instance:

Friend, for your epitaphs I'm grieved,
Where still so much is said;
One-half will never be believed,
The other never read.

His epitaph on Newton was a model:

Nature and Nature's work lay hid in night;
God said, "Let Newton be," and all was light.

If an acquaintance of yours can express himself cleverly and with an economy of words, watch for an opportunity to "make money on him." Many people have a knack for twisting some already well-known epigrams, giving them "surprise endings." This trick is always welcome if it is not off-color. The new version must sound so much like the original that it can be easily identified, yet it must be twisted to evoke laughter.

He who laughs last is an Englishman.

And a bit of parody on Shakespeare:

I dare do all that may become a man;
Who dares do more is woman.

FACT FILLER

Facts are what articles are made of, but we must be careful about recording those facts in a dull, prosaic fashion. Unless our writing is interesting and entertaining, it is unlikely to sell. "Fictionize"—"humanize"—call it what you will, the treatment we give it must have life and sparkle.

As to subject, the fact item may be about people or events in the past, present, or future. Your main concern is to select topics of general human interest, directing your choice to the type of readers you have in mind for the particular market. Even if you're able to write in a more interesting style than that which you find published, the subject you pick may bar you from its acceptance.

As to length, the fact filler can range from twenty to a few hundred words. Since every magazine to some extent publishes fact fillers, you can readily see the scope of such a market. Of course the class of the magazine governs the word rate. Not big pay, in many cases, but an astonishing boost to one's morale, and how those sales do help to solve the postage problem.

In writing the longer items, it is better to gather facts either by travel or by research, getting the information first hand. You not only have a monopoly on the subject but you can inject life into the piece possible only by your personal association with the facts.

But keep yourself out of the article. And write without prejudice. Fit the facts into their proper places. State them clearly and stop.

Now suppose I decide to submit a little fact filler to a literary magazine. An author's name is already familiar to the readers so I'll need no introductory explanation about the personality. I'll select, for instance, Robert Louis Stevenson and when I've read the facts about his life, I'm impressed with many unusual things. Even events after his death fascinate me. There is no reason, then, why I should not plunge into the subject at once and write it in a simple, matter-of-fact way.

Robert Louis Stevenson, traveler and writer of the warm seas, is buried on the summit of a hill in Samoa, to which the natives who loved him so well hewed a path and carried his body. There a tomb has been erected to his memory and to do him further homage, the chiefs have prohibited the use of firearms on the mountain so that the birds might remain there unmolested and sing around his grave.

Now then, still sticking to the subject of authors, suppose I round up a few facts about several this time and let my article take on a new look. After research I decide to deal with one experience common among those authors—the struggle to become known in the literary world. My next move is to tie in those facts with possible discouraging experiences *new* writers are facing. I gather my material, plan the arrangement and length of the article, and decide that a writer's magazine is a likely market for it. Here is one of mine that appeared some time ago.

You Who Would Write

"They who say that work hardens one, or wearies him," says novelist Edna Ferber, "have chosen the wrong profession, or have never really tasted the delights of it. It's the finest refreshener in the world." Now to many of us who have slaved at typewriters until the tenants have moved out below us; or whose eyes suffer from daily strain watching for the mailman; or whose faith is so frequently shaken by the editor's insisting that he "can find no place for our manuscripts in his present plans"— well, to us the word "refreshener" is a little out of order.

But wait a minute. Maybe that last story you wrote *did* come hard. Remember how you sat up hours later than you intended to because you couldn't leave the thing alone? And remember how pleased you were with yourself when you finally crawled in between the sheets at 3 A.M.?

How about a day or two later when the note came: *Cut this article to 1800 words and re-submit.* You dropped everything, didn't you, and just poured out your soul on it? An editor's check was in the offing. You had a real job to do, and the finished one had to click! No fooling here. You might sweat blood, but you'd *have* to come through. And it was fun, wasn't it, just to see how much you *could* do to improve it?

With that in the mail, you're reminded of that short story you wrote a year ago and couldn't sell. Which should you do, re-vamp the thing and send it out on its eighth trip, or throw it back in the files and start the one that's been germinating for two weeks? Hastily you skim through the story. Something clicks. Why, what had made you think it would sell in the first place? Funny it didn't strike you that way a long time ago. Anybody could see that the real plot dies on page six. You stand there, in awe of your new discovery, your heart pounding with excitement. You dash for the typewriter. In short order that's pounding, too. This is more like it. The whole picture is changing; new ideas are flitting as fast as the typewriter keys. Now you're beginning to see what the novelist meant: "Writing is a refreshener."

Maybe the next time, though, it wouldn't work this way. Maybe the old story should stay in the files, a subtle but effective reminder of what's wrong with your writing. Surely, though, there's hope for that article you wrote last week. Or isn't there? Well, one thing is sure: if you think you're licked, you are. So instead, why not apply for membership in one of the greatest orders among writers—the *Hang On and Don't Die* fraternity? You don't know about it? Listen.

For eight years *Booth Tarkington* wrote constantly but earned exactly $22.50. Finally a magazine editor accepted one of his stories, *Cherry*, but it was shelved as a mistake in judgment and unearthed only after the publication of *M. Beaucaire*.

Norman Douglas says his first book, *Siren Land,* "was hawked about for more than a year without success"; in fact, two other writers were instrumental in finally getting the publisher to accept it.

Louis Bromfield wrote four unpublished novels before his "first" one, *The Green Bay Tree*, was sold in 1924.

Zona Gale has always written. Yet records show that for nine years she was writing stories and submitting them persistently to the magazines before one was accepted.

Edwin Arlington Robinson, being forced to leave Harvard because of his father's long illness, continued to write poetry for two years, most of which was thrown away.

Sinclair Lewis and *William Rose Benét* lived together for six months on a borrowed hundred dollars. During that time Lewis sold one joke.

Kathleen Norris's first book, *The Colonel and the Lady,* was acepted in 1904 for $15.50. After a period of settlement work, she did newspaper reporting until one editor dismissed her, saying she could not write. Five years later she sold a short story to *Atlantic Monthly* after the manuscript had come back to her 28 times.

Julia Peterkin, whose one ambition was to play as many Beethoven sonatas as she could, related one day to her teacher as she was taking a music lesson, an incident that had just taken place on her large cotton plantation. At the completion of her story, her instructor's comment was, "You ought to write that story. You tell stories better than you play." That incident is one of the high spots in *Black April,* appearing in 1927.

These are only a small representation of the *Hang On and Don't Die* order. And there's one nice thing about it—it's an organization that's never so crowded that it can't accept new members. To be eligible, though, remember that you must have one special quality—*perseverance*—and that's accomplished only through persistent study of accepted writing, a conscientious self-analysis, and writing!

So if there's a real skeleton in your writing closet, leave it there. If, however, in that file of yours there's a story you still have faith in, one that you won't believe is unsalable, dig it out and go to work on it. Maybe you'll find after all this time that it's simply an anemic specimen. Test it. Subject it to a rigid intravenous treatment. Give it all the strength, vitality you know how. And through surgery, face-lifting, or whatever remedy is called for, rejuvenate it, make it survive. Accept the challenge of other writers' experiences. Above all, *hang on and don't die!*

The fact phase of this article could have gone on and on. There are literally dozens of other authors who have had similar experiences. We must, however, learn to judge when enough is enough. And what I have done here in the field of writing could be substituted very easily by facts concerning places, customs, historical figures, highway signs, inventions, and the like.

HOBBY ARTICLE

You can earn a good income in your spare time by writing for the hobby markets. A hobby article is nothing more than a fact article slightly fictionized to give it a realistic quality. But as in fiction, the story sense is vital. Usually it is a good idea to start the article with an anecdote that illustrates the subject and to close with one that has impact. The beginning may seem like the beginning of any short story, but the reader is soon carefully taken into the account of the hobby itself.

It is likely that every small town in America has at least one hobby enthusiast worth writing about. And if you've been following current trends, you are already aware of the appeal such articles make. In case you do not have a hobby yourself, you're still in a position to earn some easy cash by writing about those of others. Not always are these hobbies unusual; at times the emphasis lies with the person's age, or how he became interested in the project, or the remuneration received. In this field the competition can never be too great, for the world is full of people today with ingenuity and promise, all providing good subjects for hobby pieces.

Upon discovering a subject whose hobby is "good meat" for an article, you will find in most cases that he is more than willing to cooperate in giving you the necessary information. Save time for him, though, by having a list of questions ready that will give you directly and quickly the facts you need. If his hobby has developed into a full-time business, you have an even greater responsibility in relating the experiences he has had in transition.

Strangely enough, these articles do not always find the best outlets in hobby magazines. Sunday supplements, intermediate and senior-age-level church papers, as well as regular household magazines furnish an opportunity for us to sell our wares.

Every hobby article should be *good reading* first; instruction is second in importance. The narrative style is best, the complete story being simply a series of carefully arranged facts and anecdotes telling how the hobby idea originated, how first executed, length of time consumed, particular enjoyment received, and profit realized. At least one picture should accompany a hobby article.

You will find several phases of this type of writing fascinating: gathering the facts, weaving them into your "story," and showing the influence of that activity upon the person's life or even on the lives of others. Often a hobby article can go even deeper; it can reveal some inner quality of the person about whom we're writing. If we've captured that quality, and done it justice in our article, the reader will feel repaid for having read it, no matter how remote the hobby itself is from his experience.

Let me illustrate. I was acquainted with a young high school girl one time whose versatility was amazing. She could sketch practically anything that came into sight; she was a beautiful horseback rider; her scrapbook was a museum piece; she was imaginative, creative, with a good sense of values. Then one day a blow came that was to make her a cripple. In relating her story in a 1,000-word personality article, I simply culled out of her many interests the one hobby that she developed during her convalescence. This is as it appeared in a magazine for teen-agers.

His Be the Glory

That February day could have brought a permanent blight to Ruth Hanson's life had she let it. Having always been fond of out-of-door sports, she was returning with a group of young people from an ice-skating party when it happened. Seconds before she reached the front door of her home, she slipped on a tiny piece of ice and fell to the ground. Heartsick, her friends learned that the hip was so badly broken that Ruth's school days were definitely over for the year.

The customary waiting period over, Ruth was again faced with bad news. Upon removal of the cast, the doctors discovered that the fracture had not healed. Instead, the bone had begun to crumble and an immediate operation was urgent.

The months that followed could have been dull, irksome ones for anybody. Absolute quiet in the confinement of her own room spelled a still blacker picture as far as school days were concerned. But Ruth was not to be downed. She had trusted God during "good days" and had found Him not wanting. She could trust Him through this trial as well. She was at heart unselfish, so with a prayer for patience and for the ability to do something for others, Ruth dedicated those months to purposeful service.

The way was slow at first to open upon avenues other than for personal pastime. Her transistor radio—embroidery—her scrapbook—collecting poems—these filled many hours but without the feeling of achievement that Ruth craved.

One afternoon while trying to think of something different for "busy work," her mind went back to fourth grade days when she had been taught a few principles of soap carving. What a spectacle she must have made—that little awkward kid in pig-tails trying to make an igloo out of Ivory! No wonder when it was half-done, the teacher had asked her what she had decided to make! Ruth smiled. Could she do any better now? With a fresh cake of soap and a sharp razor blade, she was willing to find out.

It was only natural that Ruth's first love, her horse, should be the choice for a beginning subject. Her tools increased to a nail-file, pencil, and jack-knife. The result was more than even she had anticipated. Dogs, cats, and lambs in various moods and antics were part of her first exploits. But her finished objects did not resemble the ordinary soap-carved figures. Of an adventurous nature always, Ruth experimented with a coating of her own concoction for the final effect she wanted. In time she had conquered it. The finished products would pass anywhere for ceramic figurines.

"Ruth, when did you learn this?" her friends began to ask. "And will you make some for us?"

"We supposed soap-carved objects always looked like soap!" remarked others. "But not these!"

That was what Ruth had been waiting for. She could at least pay back her friends something of the debt she owed them for their kindness. To her collection were soon added small pedestals, crosses, a graceful figure of a woman's head, a kitten at play, and others. The little neighbor boy who came every day to her window and held up his perfect spelling paper so proudly for her inspection—she was sure he'd like a miniature Buffalo Bill.

The news spread rapidly. Would she take orders? They were ideal gifts for desks, bric-a-brac shelves, window sill decorations. Ruth was thrilled. She had been hoping to do something useful for others and here was a hobby developing into a business.

When we first interviewed Ruth, she had just finished the most difficult of her carvings. "I wanted to try a family of deer," she said, "but I wasn't sure it would work. Out of one cake I carved the doe with a fawn lying by her side. With one of the others I made the ground and stood the buck, made

of the third cake, in the middle, fastening his legs in
with melted soap. The figures finished, I fastened the
three cakes of Ivory together with melted soap chips,
pouring the liquid soap over the edges. I'm waiting
now for the solid block to dry and harden before I
can go on with the painting."

Two operations have been performed since
then, and Ruth by special home instruction, completed her tenth and all of her eleventh year. With
the aid of crutches she then returned to school for
her senior year where, as usual, she drew acclaim
for her many special talents.

As the school yearbook was being prepared, the
editorial staff began scouting among members of the
class for possible candidates to the "Who's Who"
department. It came as no surprise that Ruth was
one of those elected. By this time, however, several
other accomplishments were added to the list, among
them her beautiful work in oil painting.

As the committee congratulated her upon the
splendid use she had made of her long hours at
home, as well as for her various contributions in so
many fields, Ruth was quick to divert any credit
from herself. She had not forgotten their interest in
her during her lonely years of waiting. She was
thrilled, she said, with the discovery of a hobby that
could well mean a future for her. But most of all,
she had discovered something else. "I've learned,"
she said, "that when God takes away some things
from us, He always compensates by giving us
others."

To her friends, Ruth had won another victory.

HOW-TO ARTICLE

No matter what you are interested in personally, you can put your own experience or that of friends into the how-to filler. This category includes both the how-to-do and the how-to-make items. Maybe you are mechanically minded and you have come across some home-made gadget that can make a job simpler. Often such a little device, explained simply, can make the reader say, "Well, why didn't *I* think of that?"

Now what types of projects is the reading public interested in? Anything and everything. Things that are useful, decorative, time-saving, novel, money-saving, labor-saving. They like everything from a clever toy built for a three year old to a new model mousetrap. Particularly popular are ideas on how to use scrap material for various projects, whether of wood, metal, plastic, or cloth.

In great demand, too, are what we term "one evening projects." All magazines like them. For one thing they fill small spaces. For another, most of the readers are busily employed and would have neither the time nor access to equipment necessary to carry out a complicated project.

Seldom is a juvenile weekly published without at least one how-to article. When you consider that there are over one hundred of them published a week, you can readily see what a splendid opportunity this field of fillers alone furnishes the writer. Then add to that number all the adult magazines including *Popular Science*, *Popular Mechanics*, *Popular Homecraft*, *Hobby-Craft Magazine*, *Better Homes and Gardens*, *House and Garden*, and dozens of others. No wonder a young writer once said, "After I found that the how-to market is limitless, I've been concentrating on nothing else for weeks." Incidentally those fillers have dealt with such subjects as: How to make Christmas tree decorations out of walnut shells; a novel pin-cushion for mother; how to relax; how to shop with ease; a two-way coffee table; how to find time to read; a child's penny bag"; and many others.

A *must* in this type of filler is presentation in simple, understandable words. No fancy talk except for a sentence or two at the beginning to create attention and interest. Write only what the reader must know to build the project. The less writing, the better, so long as the explanation is clear and definitely workable. We are assuming, of course, that the object to be made or the system to be described will be ingenious enough so that the reader will be interested, yet simple enough so that he can make or do it himself.

Perhaps the method you will find most successful in writing a how-to article is the recipe style. First list in a column all the "ingredients" you're going to need in constructing the object. In another column write in order the steps necessary to build the object. Actually, many an article has started with "What you will need" for an introduction. Then when you come to directions, simply expand the second column of steps in a simple, readable, easy-to-follow procedure. Editors of juvenile magazines have endorsed this type of presentation for its clarity and conciseness.

To summarize, let me suggest three principles to follow. First, make sure that the subject you select is one you are perfectly familiar with, one that you have had or experienced yourself. Don't risk dreaming up something. Try it out and prove it to your honest satisfaction. If it's practical and worthwhile, the reader will think so, too.

Second, write the article immediately after you have carried out the project. In that way nothing of importance escapes you, and you can write the article more rapidly and accurately. After a little practice at this type of writing, you will make one discovery: that the first draft is often nearly ready to send out to an editor. I do not advocate immediate mailing, however. I have found that by letting an article "cool" while I go to another and then returning to the how-to piece, the first draft usually reveals any need for minor revision.

Third, direct every word toward making yourself crystal clear. Convince everyone reading it, including the editor, that it would be fun or profitable to try.

It is *simple* to write on a *simple* little subject if we follow a *simple formula.* Here is one that appeared in a *column* of Christmas suggestions; therefore the stimulus (attention-getting introduction) does not appear here.

Make a red apple Santa Claus for each dinner place, or at least for each child. Invert the apple, stem end down, and attach marshmallow legs by sticking a toothpick through a marshmallow and so through the apple. Make marshmallow arms the same way, pointing upward in a welcoming gesture. Then add one more marshmallow right on the top and paste to it a Santa face Christmas sticker with a red cap and a snowy white cotton beard.

To finish it off, add a shiny red cranberry on the end of each toothpick so that Santa appears to have red shoes, red mittens, and a red pompon on his cap.

As we said earlier, the how-to does not always deal with something tangible. Often we can explain some system, some time-saving methods that are equally acceptable to the public. One of the best little articles of this type that I ever saw was entitled "How a Writer Can Save Time to Write."

Frequently a whole column of "hints to housewives" is popular with editors of women's magazines. And why not? Their readers *are* looking for the very solutions that perhaps *you* have discovered to some everyday problems.

Notice the simplicity of the items printed here, and yet pooled together, they formed a portion of a one-column filler:

Broken glassware?	Melted alum is better than glue. It holds well and does not show.
Drying chamois?	They'll not dry like a board if you'll hang them in the wind or in front of a fan.
Cleaning silver?	Covering with sour milk for 30 minutes will remove tarnish. Wash and dry.
Stained washbowls?	Rub with turpentine and baking soda. Wash immediately with soap and water to kill the turpentine odor.

THE JOKE

Contributing jokes to magazines may seem like an unimaginative way to begin writing, but it *can* give you practice in putting together proper details and often trains you for one of the better-paying kinds of fillers, the anecdote.

Be sure that the joke you develop is not off-color. Popular magazines are not going to risk their reputations by publishing shady stuff. Neither will you sell it unless it's definitely amusing. All jokes must have a sharp punch line that will bring a laugh.

Someone has said, "There is no brand new joke under the sun." With the exception of remarks made out of innocence or the sly wit among our friends, that may be true. How, then, are they invented? Well, like the epigram, sometimes old jokes can be brought up to date with modern clothes. Given a new setting, new characters, or even a new situation, the material found in old almanacs and other old publications can be streamlined.

A joke is often only a question and an answer. That being the case, you need no details whatever. Here is an example, gleaned from one of the grade teachers in my home town:

> Teacher: (in health class) Bill, where are the tonsils?
> Bill: In the back of the throat behind the pilot.

A few explanatory words, sometimes one sentence,

will help you to promote the joke and still not enter it in the category of an anecdote. For example:

> The portly lady making her way along the snowy sidewalk was the target for the mischievous little fellow behind her.
> "How come you hit me in the back with that snowball?" she asked sharply.
> "That's where I aimed," he replied calmly.

LETTERS

This particular type of article is so very personal in content that there is nothing to explain. However, the market offers too attractive a reward for us to neglect mentioning it.

A glance at the requirements for letters as specified in various magazines will furnish you with the details: subject to be covered, length desired, and rate of payment.

Most of them deal with timely topics. Keep your letter brief, packed with details relevant to your subject.

THE LONGER ARTICLE

The free-lance *market* for articles continues to expand, providing a growing opportunity for the average writer. You have but to glance at the table of contents of any issue of *Reader's Digest* and note the source of the original article to sense the situation.

Not only the scope of markets but the wide variety of *subjects* developed into the longer article should serve as an incentive to the writer. The subject matter sought today covers the whole field of human interest, from homemaking to science, sports to exploration. The only requisites are that they be interesting and that they have some significance to the reader. As we have said earlier, you must be interested in the subject to write about it with zest and to spend the energy that you'll need to sell it in today's competitive market. After all, the article writer is a craftsman, an artist in his own way, and he should expect to work.

Once you have settled on a subject that interests you, make sure you do three things:

1. Keeping in mind the person who will read it, select an impressive (even perhaps compelling) and appropriate title.

2. Plan a beginning that will capture your reader's interest. It may take a clever anecdote; maybe a startling question. Whether you entertain, amuse, chide, or threaten, do *something* to bait his interest.

3. Make sure you study the magazine toward which you're aiming in order to get the "feel" of it. Is the article right for the audience you intend to have?

"Longer articles" (2,500 words and up), for want of a better name, can be classified in a variety of ways. It is not our intention in this book, however, to break them down into strict types, because several of them have so much in common that it is very difficult to draw a clearcut line. It is far more important anyhow to be interested in turning out salable articles than in learning how to label them. We shall in passing, though, mention only a few of those commonly recognized.

1. The feature article—Written to enlighten and/or entertain the reader. It contains material chosen chiefly for its human interest, not for its news value.

The information need not be recent or of great importance, but it must appeal to a large number of people. Its entertainment value comes somewhat from the subject but far more from the style.

(a) *general feature,* dealing with a subject that the public cannot withstand. For example, a unique business; the home-town boy who is succeeding in the world; hobby of a prominent person; an unusual scientific activity.

(b) *timely feature,* centered around holidays, seasons, celebrations, anniversaries.

The feature article demands no special form, but there are some very definite requirements it should meet. The chief ones are these: (1) *a striking introduction* (Attention-getting is the thing (2) *accuracy of statements* (3) *good taste* (Guard against offense to readers. Avoid oversentimentality, crudeness, satire) (4) *suitable length* (dependent upon topic) (5) *appropriate tone* (in keeping with the subject).

2. NARRATIVES

(a) *First person*

(b) *Third person*—Both of these are either personal experiences of the author or of someone he knows or perhaps a how-it-was-done article.

This type can well include all the features of good fiction: conversation, description, suspense. Emphasis here is not on *how* to do a thing but rather an entertaining piece on what *was* done.

3. Collectives—These articles consist of a number of brief items, somewhat related, and brought together for a single effect.

Often the first paragraph introduces the reader to the theme that will be carried throughout the piece and from that point on each separate item is a different opinion, viewpoint, or illustration of that theme. For instance, some time ago there appeared in one of our popular magazines an article on superstition. After one or two paragraphs of rather general facts concerning how superstitious people really are, either consciously or unconsciously, the author related the various quirks and whims of a dozen of our well-known personalities, using in several cases the exact words of those interviewed.

This type lends itself well to such topics as "What I Want for Christmas," "My Idea of Budgeting," "My Favorite Menus," opinion polls concerning certain policies, gift suggestions, etc. The style should be crisp and exact.

4. Personality Sketch (sometimes referred to as the *profile*)— In this type of article the emphasis is on the individual and his achievements. It has many of the same qualities as a hobby article, with its anecdotes revealing the personality, his quoted words, and the inclusion of both minor and major experiences that will portray him in characteristic action. Its purpose is to entertain and to inspire.

Unlike the hobby article, however, the personality sketch contains considerable detail. The reader must be given an accurate word picture of the personality. To accomplish this one must include bio-graphical data, physical characteristics, habits, man-nerisms, and his general interests in life—obtainable to the writer by means of the interview and/or per-sonal acquaintance. Always seek the opinion of others, as well, about the individual. By nature the reader audience is a curious one; it is interested in learning what others think, believe, feel. We must satisfy that curiosity, then, by furnishing a complete picture.

5. THE INTERVIEW—The purpose in this type of article is to let the reader know what the personality is like by what he *says*; therefore, most of the content of an interview is furnished by the individual himself, and the writer's responsibility is to record the fur-nished facts accurately.

We do not necessarily have to fill the piece with quotations, but the article should present some of the quoted words of the one interviewed. Since his personal opinions form an important part of the article, you can see why direct quotes are most de-sirable. To support those statements, bits of bio-graphical data can well be introduced.

Much preliminary work on the part of the writer should be done before an interview is sought. One should have a basic knowledge of the personality, his education, training, achievements. Furthermore, the writer should prepare a list of questions to ask the individual, both to save time and to promote orderliness of detail. Above all, he should be tactful in his approach. To inquire in advance for an ap-pointment is, of course, a must, explaining what he would like to do with the information if the person is willing.

The article itself is best written in third person, resembling a narrative.

6. ESSAYS—Essay articles are among the most popular among editors today. They can be of many varieties —informational, explanatory, humorous, even argumentative. Actually they offer many possibilities to the less experienced writer because the emphasis lies not in a masterful style but in an interesting presentation of material.

In this field the writer has a chance to voice arguments against issues of wide interest; he can air his "pet peeves"; he can defend his position or opinion in a humorous way. His purpose is to make the reader think as he does, to change the reader's point of view. If it is a serious theme, he must make sure he has all the facts and that they are arranged in an order that would bring weight enough to influence the reader.

The wise writer will use the same techniques as in stories. He will catch the reader with the opening paragraph, make him stay with him through a series of incidents, and leave him with a feeling of regret that the article had to end.

The tone of the essay article will depend upon the vein intended—serious or humorous. Almost by the title you can determine the mood of a piece and discover how everyday material can be put to use easily by those who can see the commonplace in a new light.

Notice some of these titles that were picked at

random from household magazines. We're sure they will set you to thinking of subjects that you, too, could dream up.

"18 Ways to Make Yard Work Easier"; "Your Attic May Be Your Future"; "How to Live Happily Without a Maid"; "Ask the Birds Over"; "Bees Can Make Your Sugar"; "Is Your Youngster Slow to Talk?"; "Fun for Everyone" (at-home games for the family); "Put Pattern Into Your Garden"; "How Good a Parent Are You?"; "A Dozen Don'ts That Save Lives"; "Do Things With Your Children"; "Diary of a Desperate Daddy"; "We Raised the Roof" (for a remodeled attic room); "What to do for the Shy Child"; "Are You Fit to Visit the Sick?"

The question sometimes arises: "Is it better to use a name other than one's own when submitting articles, and if so, what is the advantage?" Let me inject a thought here concerning "by-lines." Sometimes, not often, there is a really good reason for deviating from one's established name. In everything pertaining to sports, for instance, or out-of-door adventures, most editors wish it to appear that those articles have been prepared by male authors. Now if the author of an accepted piece is "Mary Jo Halsey," she may find that when the work is published, the author will be listed as "M. J. Halsey" or "Joe Halsey." Many women writers can adapt themselves to a male point of view, especially in humorous writing. It would be crazy to expect a nod from an editor unless the woman had used a masculine "by-line." Likewise, the male writer in "borrowing" a woman's theme.

There is, of course, at least one other good reason for pen names. More than once the editor of a monthly magazine has carried two articles by the same author, unaware of his true identity. Obviously, the writer gets two checks instead of one.

But to get back to the essay. Of the six types of articles we have discussed here, none can offer the writer any more liberty than this informal one. And if he can add a little humor to whatever he's writing, that is, of course, even better. Readers appreciate an opportunity to laugh or smile, and editors, aware that the American public seeks to be amused, welcome well-written and genuinely humorous pieces.

There are several ways a writer can appeal to his audience. He can take them off guard by giving a subtle treatment to an otherwise thought-provoking subject. He can create a ludicrous situation out of one that the reader has already taken for granted. He can impersonate and imitate. He can reminisce. He can even yield to broad satire.

These "gimmicks" are not new. Frank Colby was thriving fifty years ago because he had learned how to write wittingly on women's hats, or on his bouts with a foreign language, or on poor story tellers. Ring Lardner of the same era was constantly working himself out of some dilemma while his readers were convulsed at the improbable solutions he offered. Clarence Day, Finley Peter Dunne, and later James Thurber, Cornelia Otis Skinner, and many others have capitalized on the informal article because of its general reader appeal.

Throughout the years household magazines have been especially good markets for these articles—*The American Home, Better Homes and Gardens, Good Housekeeping, Woman's Day* to name a few. As one editor said, "Their popularity was demonstrated several decades ago, and since human nature doesn't change, our attitude toward the light vein essay won't either."

We have selected here for illustration one that was written many years ago. For some of our readers there may be a slightly nostalgic response; others, who are familiar only with present-day cleaning methods, may react differently. Our chief purpose, of course, is to demonstrate how one can get humor out of the commonplace.

I'm a Fugitive From a Dustpan [1]
C. Ford

There's one thing I just don't understand about women. Wait a minute! I guess I'd better start this article all over again.

There are a *whole lot* of things I don't understand about women, and one of them is why they always speak of "spring housecleaning." Anything that starts on the morning of March 22 and ends at midnight on March 21 the following year certainly doesn't deserve to be called "spring." Any more than what they do to a house deserves to be called "cleaning." Any more than what's left of the house after they finish deserves to be called a "house."

It wouldn't be so bad if they'd really *clean* and get done; but they just keep pushing the dust around from one place to the other, apparently on the theory that sooner or later it'll get lost.

In this regard, a Professor Fracker of Harvard conducted a rather interesting experiment in his own house recently. He took a piece of dust, marked it

[1] Reprinted from *Better Homes & Gardens* magazine. By permission of Meredith Publishing Company.

carefully with a bit of red string, and deposited it on a closet shelf. The following morning, after his wife had finished cleaning, he found the piece of dust on the floor under the bureau. Two mornings later, after his wife had dusted under the bureau, he discovered the same piece of dust downstairs in the living room behind a picture of his wife's mother. During the following week, it showed up successively underneath the kitchen stove, inside the radio, and finally lodged on the leaf of a large *aspidistra* plant in the front hall. The only way he got rid of it at last was to sweep it up himself and exhibit it triumphantly to his wife, as a result of which the piece of dust was thrown out the front door, closely followed by Professor Fracker.

Each spring, about the time the first crocus flies north, a strange fanatic gleam appears in the average woman's eye. Thoughtfully she wets her finger and runs it along the top of a shelf, peers at the tip, and murmurs to herself, "Hmmm." To an inexperienced male, this may not seem like anything to get alarmed about; but to a wary veteran of countless housecleanings, such as the battered author of this article, it's as clear cut a warning as though she's blown a bugle in his ear. His cue is to tiptoe upstairs right then and there, pack his suitcase, and move out for six months or so until the ordeal is over.

For some reason, the housecleaning urge is something no woman can resist. Despite the fact that it may be the kind of house in which you can eat right off the floor—and once she starts cleaning, that's just the kind of house it *will* be—she'll seize on the least excuse to tie a towel around her head, grab a broom, and indulge in a vernal orgy of sweeping, beating, scrubbing, and general mayhem that would make a full-scale blitzkrieg seem like a quiet afternoon nap under the Sunday papers. The harried male develops a reflex action in time. The very first whine of a vacuum cleaner, like the sound of a dentist's drill, produces a shiver, his toes curl inside his shoes, his hands grasp the sides of his chair, and beads of perspiration stand out on his forehead. At the first rasp of a broom across the floor, his hair stands straight on end.

There are several rather pathetic ruses which a male will employ in order to stall off the inevitable. One is to pretend ignorance of what's going on by sitting in his easy chair while his wife trudges up and down with her arms full of books, occasionally glancing up from his paper to murmur in a surprised voice: "Why didn't you ask me to help you with those, dear?" Another is to take a can of sardines and a few crackers, lock himself in his bedroom, and barricade the door with a couple of chairs and the bureau. Another is to roll himself up quietly inside a rug and let himself be carried out of the house feet first by the men from the cleaning company. Still another is to place the house on the market at once, and buy another house that is already cleaned.

All these ruses have one thing in common. They don't work.

For one thing, spring cleaning strikes without warning. The unsuspecting husband awakens in the morning, for example, amid pleasantly familiar surroundings. Everything is right where it ought to be. His bed is underneath him where it belongs, the easy chair where he sits to put on his socks has not budged an inch, his trousers are still in the middle of the floor where he hung them last night. Downstairs his chair is in its usual place at the dining-room table, his egg is in its usual place on his vest, and his wife is in her usual place opposite him with a bright smile on her face. She doesn't even complain when he drops some cigarette ashes in their usual place on the dining-room rug. "It doesn't matter, dear," she murmurs, "I'm going to clean today, anyway." He folds his newspaper, tilts up his wife's chin with his forefinger and kisses her good-by in the usual place, and sets out for the 8:19, serene in the conviction that his home will always be a permanent little haven of refuge in a changing world.

His first impression when he returns to his little haven of refuge that evening is that a cyclone has arrived to spend the weekend. The place is a shambles. The entire yard is littered with furniture, curtains and draperies hang from the clotheslines, and in the rear the maid is beating the living-room rug with his pet four-ounce Hardy fly rod. Carpets flap at him from the second story, mops and brooms bristle from every window, vacuum cleaners snarl belligerently. The front door has been removed from its hinges, and a couple of total strangers are lugging his favorite easy chair out onto the lawn. As he hurries past them through the vestibule, he trips over a large sullen woman whom he never saw before in his life, kneeling at the foot of the stairs with a pail and scrubbing brush. Removing his foot from the pail, he wanders dazed from room to room, lifting sheets and peering at the heaps of furniture beneath, trying in vain to discover a single familiar object amid all the confusion. Panic stricken, he turns and bolts upstairs (having paused first to make sure the stairs are still there) and collides head on with his wife, who is emerging from a bedroom with a cheerful smile.

"Just in time, dear," she greets him, "to start in on the attic."

To be sure, a modern method of cleaning a house is to proceed with one room at a time. Not only does this avoid tearing up the whole house at once, but it takes about ten times as long. According to this method, all the furniture is removed from one room and placed in a second room while the first one is being cleaned. Then the furniture is moved from this second room to a third room, while the second is being cleaned. Then it is moved to a fourth room while the *third* room is being cleaned. By a little careful planning on the part of the wife, the furniture will thus make a complete tour of the entire house, including a short detour by way of the neighbor's yard because the back stairs are too narrow, before it winds up again where it started from, just in time for next year's house-cleaning. For example, a large horsehair sofa in our own house covered a distance of four and six-tenth miles last spring alone. I know, because I happened to be walking under it at the time.

A friend of mine, a man named Twitchell, has a system he always uses when his wife asks him to lug around furniture like this. His system, which is known as the Twitchell System, is really very simple. All he does, when spring housecleaning is about to start, is to fill an ordinary smudge pot with autumn leaves, old rags, and pieces of rubber tire, and touch a match to it in the front hall. He then flings open the windows and shouts "Fire!" After that, he just stands by and watches his neighbors carry out all his furniture for him. He usually has to carry it back all by himself, though.

Not only can a husband be useful to his wife in little ways like lugging furniture. If time hangs heavy on his hands, for instance, he may be drafted to beat the mattress. The husband tries at first to make a little game of this, by pretending the mattress is Hitler. After a while his enthusiasm palls, but he gets a new burst of energy by pretending it is the Emperor of Japan. By this time his back is aching, his legs are hollow, and his arms are like lead, and he keeps on going only by pretending it is his leading business rival who just snatched a big account right out from under his nose. Just as he reaches the point of collapse, however, he thinks of the person who invented spring housecleaning, and finishes beating the mattress in no time at all.

Nor does the end of housecleaning itself mean that his troubles are over. After the excitement has subsided, and the invading army of cleaning women shoulder their mops and march away, he opens his eyes and blinks on a strange and unfamiliar world. Nothing in the house is the same. No object is in its usual place any more. Everything has changed. His bed has been moved; his bureau is on the other side of the room now, away from the mirror; the comfortable chair where he used to sit and put on his socks has been replaced by a small table, and the ash tray that was always beside it has disappered entirely.

The prized photograph of the record salmon he caught in 1937 has gone, and in its place is a chrome that used to hang in the spare room, showing a castle with an orange moon and between 15 and 20 nymphs. The bedside reading lamp is missing, and the cherished books he always kept by his pillow have yielded to a series of completely strange tomes, including a couple of bound volumes of *St. Nicholas*, a book of salad recipes, and an unopened copy of *Quo Vadis*, a surprise wedding gift.

Even his closet has been straightened out, and it is physically impossible to locate any of his clothes any more. (He never *does* find his old fishing pants.) With increasing misgivings, he opens the door of his gun-room, takes one look inside, and closes the door again with a faint moan. He wanders downstairs, past brand-new curtains and unfamiliar lamps and hostile tables, and sinks down automatically in the spot usully occupied by his favorite leather chair in front of the fireplace. He lands flat on the floor with a crash. He gives his wife one reproachful look, and shuts his eyes. . . .

And there is nothing a man can do about it when the housecleaning fever grips a woman in the spring. Take my wife, for instance. (I knew we'd get around to her before this article was over.) This year, as the fatal time drew near, I resolved upon a sly plan of my own. First I managed to persuade her to take a vacation for a week and visit her cousin in Sandusky, Ohio. I saw her safely onto the train myself, kissed her good-by, and then rushed to the phone. I called in every professional cleaner in the city. I hired a flying wedge of women with mops. I even got the local fire department to help. In the course of that week, we went over that house from top to bottom. We turned it inside out, and removed every last particle of dust. We beat all the rugs, scrubbed the floors, washed the windows, polished the bathrooms, and scoured the basement. When the week was over, every nook and corner of the place shone like a mirror. I met my wife at the train on her return and led her home triumphantly. "Well," I beamed, as she entered the house, "and how does it look?"

She paused a moment in the hall, a strange far-off look in her eye. Thoughtfully she wet her finger and ran it along the top of the hall table, peered at the tip, and murmured to herself: "Hmmm . . ."

That is why the typing of this article may seem a little shaky. At the present moment I am seated on a pile of books in the center of the floor, using a portable typewriter that is propped on the horse-hair sofa. A vacuum-cleaner cord is twined around my feet, a strange woman with a pail and scrubbing brush is advancing toward me slowly on her hands and knees, and two men have just started to pick up the sofa and carry it into the next room.

I think that's my wife you hear calling me now.

THE PUZZLE

Perhaps you have never thought of puzzle construction as any part of the writing business. Perhaps you are unaware of the sales opportunities the field really offers. If you like to construct things, though, you may find that crosswords and other types can serve as fill-ins between articles while those "idea bugs" are germinating. Let me illustrate. I toyed with a juvenile picture crossword one time and became so engrossed in it that I finished three before going on to something else. I traced the outlines and cross lines in India ink and almost out of curiosity sent them to a juvenile magazine editor. Within a few days I received word that she not only wanted those three but a year's supply! The idea I had toyed with was bringing me $5 for each three by four inch space.

Months later when I hit a "dry spell," I constructed another dozen and sold them to a juvenile magazine distributed in public schools. A third publisher saw them and sensing the educational value for children as well as the enjoyment, requested that I sign a contract at once for a year's supply.

With about two dozen puzzle magazines on the market, as well as books coming out in series, the puzzle market has today grown large enough and steady enough to provide hundreds of people with a means of extra income. The field is not hard to break into; it does provide fun and profit.

Like everything else, there are rules to follow if we expect to submit standard crosswords that will be acceptable.

1. Study published diagrams, both the original ones and their answers. You will see that each contains an odd number of squares in both directions and that those sizes are thirteen by thirteen (the most popular), fifteen by

fifteen, seventeen by seventeen, nineteen by nineteen, or twenty-one by twenty-one.

2. Notice that each puzzle is symmetrical—that is, it contains a balanced pattern with corresponding black squares in opposite sides. Usually the filled-in squares occupy no more than one-sixth of the total number.

3. Start with a diagram in one of the papers or magazines you have. Since the same designs are used over and over (because only the words are copyrighted), construct your first puzzle with an already established design.

4. In your first attempts at making your *own* puzzles, use a thirteen by thirteen square and see that the design is a very simple one containing a large number of black squares. Also design it so that the corner words will contain no more than three or four letters.

5. Usually it is best to begin in the upper left corner, working down and across, and concentrating on the longer words as you do so. Since they are the hardest, as you progress from the upper left corner down to the center, make sure the long words are correct.

6. Do not repeat a word in the puzzle. Leave no square unkeyed.

7. After you have filled out a number of diagrams and are getting the "feel" of construction, begin work on the definitions. Avoid a sameness and dullness in them. By studying the published ones from several sources, you

will observe a rather lively and informative definition used.

8. Your equipment should consist of at least one standard dictionary, a crossword dictionary, crossbar paper, and some sharp pencils.

9. When submitting them do one of two things: (1) Draw your design on eight and a half by eleven white bond and fill in black squares solidly with India ink, or (2) purchase ready-made forms (fifteen by fifteen) for about $1.50 per hundred. Always use capital letters. Definitions should be on a second sheet of bond, following the plan of most published puzzles.

Here is one of the first picture crosswords I sold:

Vertical

1 A breed of dogs (pl)
2 Dogs kept to play with
5 A dog's foot (pl)
8 Reared
9 Fairy
11 Dry
12 Vestment worn by clergy
14 Linger
18 What dogs love to do
19 To yield
23 Part of verb "to be"
24 Pronoun referring to self

Horizontal

3 Metal
4 Threshold rug
5 What small dogs are kept in (pl)
6 How dogs speak
7 West Africa (abbr)
8 To exist
10 Growls
13 Angry
15 Help
16 First two letters of common dog's name
17 North Dakota (abbr)
18 A narrative poem
20 A strong strap for leading dogs
21 The dog can't run when he is this
22 Rich part of milk
25 Masculine pronoun
26 Pronoun referring to self

But crosswords, despite their popularity in daily papers and periodicals, are not the only type of puzzle that sells. Religious papers, children's magazines, and school publications often carry other types that are good exercise for the reader (both juvenile and adult) and a challenge to the writer.

Puzzle construction is a field that invites ingenuity and specific information. It is fascinating and contagious. If *your* success resembles that of many others, your chief difficulty will be to *stop*.

Here are a few other types that have been received very well.

FLOWER HUNT

Hidden among the squares are the names of fourteen flowers. See how many you can find by moving to the right, to the left, up and down, but *not* diagonally. Answers: aster; rose; lily; peony; violet; pansy; hyacinth; daffodil; iris; tulip; lilac; geranium; narcissus; arbutus

A	S	R	O	L	Y	N	P
U	T	E	S	I	L	O	E
L	I	P	A	T	E	I	V
H	Y	S	N	S	I	R	L
C	A	I	A	D	A	L	T
I	N	S	R	B	C	E	G
H	T	U	T	U	I	R	C
D	O	F	D	M	N	A	I
I	L	F	A	S	U	S	S

THE WHEEL OF NAMES

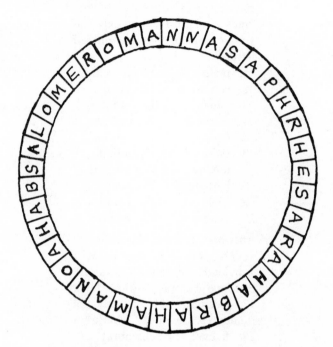

This wheel contains eighteen names found in the Bible, ranging from three to seven letters in length. See how many of them you can find, starting anywhere in the circle.

Answers: Sarah; Ahab; Rhesa; Rahab; Noah; Abraham; Raham; Ham; Haman; Anna; Manoah; Absalom; Salome; Merom; Roman; Annas; Asa; Asaph

FUN WITH FABRICS

Below are the names of twenty kinds of cloth. How quickly can you re-arrange these scrambled letters?

1.	ineln	11.	ignmahg
2.	simuln	12.	kuhc
3.	eliov	13.	eresukscre
4.	epralce	14.	yagonrd
5.	egers	15.	iytidm
6.	sacrh	16.	edimn
7.	noyln	17.	kinksrash
8.	baragiend	18.	nealnlf
9.	ronlo	19.	hyamcarb
10.	neotnecr	20.	techivo

Answers: 1. linen 2. muslin 3. voile 4. percale 5. serge 6. crash 7. nylon 8. gabardine 9. orlon 10. cretonne 11. gingham 12. huck 13. seersucker 14. organdy 15. dimity 16. denim 17. sharkskin 18. flannel 19. chambray 20. cheviot

THE QUIZ

Quizzes are not only fun to write but pay well for time and effort involved. As in the case of all fillers, you must study the various magazines that publish them and analyze the type used by each.

Some editors like short, snappy introductions. Others prefer very simple directions. But in the *body* of the quiz, whether it is for one of the digests or for a weekly story paper for children, the *game element* must definitely be present.

There are at least three essential factors that enter into salable quizzes: (1) a worthwhile idea (2) an interesting and easy-to-follow form and (3) a catchy title.

In Chapter Two I referred to a simple little quiz that flashed into my mind as a result of reading a magazine. Here is the way it was published.

What's In a Name?

Though it is a well-known fact that Chicago is called "the windy city" and Philadelphia "the city of brotherly love," how well can you identify these other cities by their nicknames?

Score 5 points for each correct answer.

Hub of the Universe
Railroad City
Queen City of the Lakes
City of the Straits
The Rose City
Quaker City
Crescent City
Empire City
Mile High City
Rubber City
Flour City
Pittsburgh of the South
Oil Capital of the World
City of the Angels
Golden Gate City

On another page, of course, appeared the answers: Boston; Indianapolis; Buffalo; Detroit; Portland, Ore; Philadelphia; New Orleans; New York; Denver; Akron; Minneapolis; Birmingham; Tulsa; Los Angeles; San Francisco.

QUOTES

Many of our most widely circulated general magazines scatter quotations from the writings of famous authors throughout their pages. Frequently there appear also witty or thoughtful statements by politicians, educators, scientists, and others, which you have read. Even some of the matchless truths of the Bible appear as fillers.

You see, none of these are original on *your* part and yet there is a very good chance for a sale if, searching for a half-dozen witty, perhaps seasonal, but at least opportune sayings, you can neatly compile material that the busy editor is on the lookout for.

Undoubtedly Mark Twain's pungent remarks have been quoted as frequently as those of any writer. Lincoln, too, is as popular today as he was a century ago in his comments.

This one of Mark Twain's has appeared many times: "Man is the only animal that blushes, or needs to."

RECIPE

The very word may frighten a male writer, but it need not do so. Recipes are always in demand. Sometimes just one added ingredient to an old recipe can completely transform and improve the product. "Mistakes" may mean "breaks" if we utilize them in writing.

Be sure that the opening sentence is as attractive as the food you want to "sell." Be sure also that the recipe is accurate and that the explanation that follows is clear. Place emphasis within the recipe on any good angle such as the nutritional value, time-saving factor, economy, or ease in serving.

Often newspapers and magazines run recipe contests in which they specify *new, made-over,* or *new uses* for special products. Be sure that you are original in these cases. Editors are on the watch for stolen material and it's surprising how quickly they can detect it.

RELIGIOUS FILLERS

Upon first thought you might not have regarded the religious market suitable for fillers. But these publications use many every week, some ranging from anecdotal length to 2,000 words.

Often these fillers take the form of short, religious meditations; sometimes, bits of poetry; again, news items and anecdotes with a religious tie-in. Short though these pieces are, they deserve the best wording, the most careful thought a writer can produce. They are good training for any type of writing.

A neighbor brought in a picture one day that she had taken of a winter scene. Somehow it suggested just everything one could expect of the season. I quickly asked permission to use the negative, had it enlarged to a five by seven gloss print, and hastened to write just what I saw in the picture. This was the "caption" that accompanied it when it had been prepared as a religious filler.

A dark grey cloud,
A windy day,
Snow falling fast
On fields of gray.
Deepening drifts,
Sun sitting cold;
Tall pines creaking—
Much too bold.
Ice-filled rivers,
Glistening trees;
God's own picture
Of winter are these.

The meditation type of religious filler often takes the form of some challenge, reminder, or question. These can be presented even in the style of an acrostic. For example:

	S	alvation
	A	ll
	V	ictory
Is Christ Your	I	ntercessor
	O	ffering
	U	pholder
	R	esurrection

Here is an example of a religious anecdote, published first in a newspaper as a fact item:

Mrs. Haines of .... says she always had faith in God. But today she has even more.

Nearing her home in a Colorado city one night, she was approached by a young man who brandished what appeared to be a gun and demanded her purse. In it Mrs. Haines was carrying a rather sizable sum of money for her daughter's wedding.

Her heart seemed to stand still for a moment. Then with all the calmness she could muster, she began quoting the Twenty-third Psalm: "The Lord is my shepherd; I shall not want. . . . Surely goodness and mercy shall follow me all the days of my life. . . ."

"O.K., ma'am," the fellow said. "I guess you're right." And he disappeared into the darkness.

We must not overlook the fact that the so-called religious press calls for a wide variety of material fitting into the article field: historical pieces, biographies, organizational articles, general and how-to, poetry, etc. Good articles are always needed. Some editors want secular material with a religious slant; others demand a balance between them. Practically anything is of interest.

SELF-HELP ARTICLE

There is an exceptionally wide appeal for articles dealing with personal improvement. A wide scope of subjects is also apparent.

Have you found a sure way to enjoy your *second* child that you didn't know with the first? Wife, have you discovered how to keep your husband good-natured during house-cleaning days? Husband, have you helped your wife overcome fear of water? Has either of you solved a financial, emotional, or mental problem? If you have, these are bases for several good articles.

Perhaps you haven't any experiences that you think

would fit into the self-help category. But maybe you've observed certain qualities in your friends and neighbors that would be the very outlet for that writing urge. Whatever the subject, the self-help article should follow the anecdotal style. The mood should be one of inspiration and encouragement. The article should be written simply, in straight-line logic, but giving its reader a lift and a feeling of "She's right. I'll try it."

I have found it possible to use material from my own experiences as well as from those of my friends. I believe you can, too. One article, "And Gladly Teach," was the result of my classroom "technique" at enjoying fun and accomplishment at the same time. Another article, "And They Shall Lead," was written about a family's experience with children's reading. Both were too long to print here.

Perhaps a list of some self-help article titles that have already appeared will serve to prove what a wide variety of topics you, too, can seek in this field: "Insuring a Vacation"; "Driving in Traffic"; "The Power of Faith"; "Living on $3.00 a Day"; "Staying Young"; "Correct English at Home"; "Advice to Those Who Want to Attain Eighty"; "I'm Different"; "Sincerity is What Counts."

As we have pointed out before, study the magazine that you think your article is suited to. If the self-help is regularly a one-pager, you only show that you haven't really studied the magazine if you send in a long article, regardless of how suitable the topic.

Assuming you know your material is right for the market, by studying the staff-written pieces you can decide what approach the editor prefers. Notice whether the articles start with a problem. Observe whether the introduction is usually in anecdotal style. Then look at the ending. Is it tied in with the beginning? Is it a challenge? Are you impelled to act? Judge your own work accordingly. Remember above all, that the most important thing is having something to say that will interest your readers and your editor.

TRADE JOURNAL ITEMS

Those who have really made a business of writing trade journal items have found that the sales possibilities are about as *sure* a thing as any type of filler; in fact, most of them will say that they are the *best*. These items are written about successful merchandizing ideas or about news that affects an industry as a whole. You can readily see, then, that if the idea behind the trade news item concerns *man's personal gain,* the editor of such magazines will already be aware of his readers' interest and will be quick to grab such an item.

Undoubtedly you have among your acquaintances a plumber, a druggist, a sporting goods dealer, a groceryman. Ask any one of them to let you borrow his trade journal; or if you prefer, write for a sample copy. Study the style of the articles published.

Get in conversation with the businessmen. Find out what schemes they have employed to save steps, increase business, make their places more attractive. Maybe a remodeling job is going on. Look it over. Talk with those directly concerned.

The nice part of writing for trade journals is this: Once you pick up an idea from a business friend, and write up the item, the idea can be used for at least two dozen *other* magazines. All you have to do is to slant toward the others, making sure there is no overlapping. Trade journal editors do not care if an author sells the same story to a noncompetitive publication. A story for a rug journal could be just as vital if sent to one for dealers in silverware. One filler writer told me she had sold a hundred items dealing with ideas she picked up on *one store* conversion program. We referred to this type of thing in Chapter One when we mentioned duplicating checks.

Business papers buy about 65,000 articles a year. The rate of pay varies and the editors are very, very good to beginning writers. For weekly income and for another form of writing that's enjoyable, the trade journal item is a good starter.

The contacts with businessmen can often furnish results beyond our expectations. Let me illustrate.

While buying groceries one morning in a chain store, I congratulated the newly-appointed manager and extended my good wishes for his business success. Some two months later I had an opportunity to talk with him at length about his work for I had known from the beginning that he was deeply concerned about store conditions and the volume of business when he took over. What he told me about his personal efforts to win customers inspired me to ask permission to write an item for a trade journal. He promptly loaned me a copy of the journal he subscribed to so that I might get the style in mind. To my amazement I found in that issue an announcement of a contest called "How Do You Win Customers?" and the deadline for submission was still three weeks away.

When I realized that the very things the manager had just told me would be fitting for the contest entry,

6. What are popular markets for hobby articles?
7. What types of articles *must* be accompanied by ~~ures~~ or sketches?
8. What two types of fillers make up the how-to ~~?~~
9. What is the "recipe" style?
~~.0.~~ What three things should one keep in mind when ~~·aring~~ quizzes?
~~1.~~ In what different ways do religious fillers appear?
~~2.~~ What is the main object of a trade journal item?

~~·ESTIONS~~—1. In a loose-leaf notebook (or your already ~~·lished~~ file) record (a) bright sayings from children, ~~·a~~ list of hobbyists you are acquainted with, (c) a list ~~·ojects,~~ no matter how simple, that you are capable ~~·ing,~~ and (d) any others that interest you particularly.
Form a daily habit of scouting for expressions and ~~·~~ that you can use for future writing projects. These ~~grow~~ toward a gold mine of reference material if you ~~·ersistent.~~

I quickly sought permission to submit my article but in this case to use *his* name.

Here is the entry that won the cash prize, judges at the same time commending "him" for simplicity, earnestness of efforts, and genuineness of tone in relating the story.

I was recently made manager of a small unit of our chain, and since it was a promotion that came after an unusually short length of service, I was naturally very eager to prove that I was capable of handling the work. I set myself at once to achieve two results: satisfied customers and an increased business.

I had been conscious of the lack of personal contact between my predecessor and the people who traded in our store. I was determined to do better. Not that I expected to join every organization in the town, visit homes, or throw big parties. I felt that I could do less and still make people *want* to come into my store.

The people I knew best in the community, of course, were those easiest to contact, and by spending a little time and effort in soliciting their interest, I found little trouble in listing them among my regular customers. But to reach those whom I scarcely knew, those one-day-a-week shoppers whose business I wanted, was my problem. I conceived the idea of writing a letter that would explain my position as a new manager and would present frankly the goal I had set for myself. I did not ask for their sole patronage, nor did I bait them with prizes. The letter was written simply to open the way to my store and the invitation was a cordial, sincere one.

It took time to write the letters, but since I wished to approach prospective customers in as personal a way as possible, I avoided a stereotyped form letter. It paid.

During the following month 92% of the people on my list were in the store and business showed a 30% increase. I repeated the experiment, this time on a larger scale. The result was an increase in sales of 42%.

I might add that through my efforts I have just been awarded by my company a $100 prize in a contest for increased sales. Let me say to all managers, especially those just assuming the responsibility of a store, make a friend and win a customer. It sometimes takes but a postage stamp.

Needless to say, the check was *my* remuneration, not his.

THE TRIBUTE

The tribute is sometimes thought of as an editorial, but the distinction between them definitely prevents their being synonymous.

An editorial can be an article setting forth the praises or merits of a person or project; but it *can* be equally effective to stir the public to action by the author's scornful or wrathful attack upon some shame-provoking menace.

The *tribute* means just what it says. It is a one-pager acclaiming some public figure, anniversary event, or invention. It emphasizes merits, not flaws.

Here is one I wrote on Lincol
picture of him furnished by the ma

Abraham Lincoln, Belo

No truer tribute was eve
General Grant when he said:
the nation lost its greatest her

A humble log cabin coul
of such a man. From rail-splitt
resolve alone swayed his bei
and country nobly and well
such vision, his courage was a
steadfast, yet the kindliness o
The horrors of war weighe
fought with firmness for the
thetic, compassionate, yet his
not be perverted.

Lincoln's place in histo
man *of* the people and *for* th
life and gave it ungrudgingl
heroism is denied us.

THINGS TO DO

PERSONAL INVENTORY—1. Why are
attractive to the writer than joke

2. Where can anecdotes be

3. What is the beginning wr
writing an anecdote?

4. What forms can an epigr

5. Where does one look for
article?

CHAPTER FOUR

The Touch that Sells

Long ago when Ben Jonson wrote, "A good poet's made as well as born," he could just as well have included writers of fillers and articles. In fact, "born writers" are few and there's a thirty-to-one chance you're not one of them. Like most people, you will probably have to learn how to write by a trial-and-error method.

Some, unfortunately, are happy once they have finished page one regardless of what is on it. Others ask how they can avoid writing about twice the amount they intended. Still others reach a fork in the road, are uncertain which one to take, and end up so differently from their original intentions that the piece is an utter failure. In each case the writer has not learned a vital lesson.

When you decide to take a week's vacation and visit a section of the country you've never seen, the first logical thing you do is to consult a map and route that trip. You find out which way is best, total distance to be covered, what scenic spots to look for on the way, and plan your activities within the week you've given yourself. You have a fairly good idea just what can be accomplished in those seven days. In other words, you have a plan.

HAVE A PLAN!

Writers seeking early sales could well apply this simple little illustration to their writing experience:

Use the *map*	Correct approach
Decide *route*	Type of filler
Distance	Approximate length
Scenic spots	Anecdotes or illustrations
Progress	Outline
Destination	Climax

WRITE THAT PLAN OUT!

The second step is to write the *plan* (or outline) out, not the article. It is so easy to formulate in your mind the starting point, the "scenic spots" along the way, the destination. It is not so easy, unless the plan is an itemized outline on a scrap of paper, to "drive in" where you expect to stop. No matter how simple the subject you have chosen, if it's worth writing about at all, it's worth developing in logical order and brought to an ending that doesn't make the editor flinch.

A similar formula was mentioned in the discussion of the anecdote. And even the simple joke can be poorly written if not arranged in orderly sequence. Certainly we need not add that it is imperative for fillers of greater length and complexity.

Do some specific routing. Think out the article; put down the main thoughts into sentences. Decide the order of these thoughts and write them in logical sequence. Then write the ending. You will find that proper paragraphing will take care of itself if you have planned your work carefully and minutely enough.

WHAT IS GOOD WRITING?

As we pointed out in the early part of the book, good writing is that which has come alive because the author has learned to communicate his feelings with those of his reader. He has something to say and he has made it pleasurable for us to listen to him. He has learned to eliminate trivia and by skillful treatment of facts to concentrate only on details that make the thing worthwhile. His writing will have a smoothness about it, a gliding from one portion to the next with a graceful, easy transition. You'll not have to work with the author; he has drawn you into the net of interest and you're willing to stay there.

HOW CAN WE WRITE EFFECTIVELY?

Effective writing involves (1) the use of familiar words and (2) the use of sentence variety. When writing produces clear perceptions in the minds of readers and when the tone is in keeping with the type of article and reader audience, it is effective writing.

Since clarity is the keynote to sales, our language should be simple, direct, unadorned. At the same time we should be careful to choose the *exact* word and to be satisfied with nothing less. We must avoid worn-out expressions. Surely we have had enough of "green with envy"—"meek as Moses"—"a sea of faces"—"tall sentinels on the lawn" and many others.

Let's remember that Abraham Lincoln used fewer than three hundred words in the finest address we can find in literature. In that single paragraph few words have more than two syllables. Like Lincoln, let's keep our writing simple and to the point.

Vary sentences in both *length* and *structure*. Our diet would soon become a drudge if we ate the same type of food at every meal. The suit or dress we wear loses its attractiveness if we wear it every day of the week. Even the route to work becomes tiresome because of its commonness. And so it is with paragraph composition unless we deliberately become *sentence conscious*. The length of sentences we can take care of by using our eyes. The second, working for structure variety, demands more attention.

Here are several devices for gaining sentence variety in structure:

1. Avoid successive sentences beginning with the subject.

> Poor: The summer had long since drawn to a close. An ominous transformation had taken place in the landscape. The forest glowed like a bed of tulips. The painted foliage reflected a variety of colors.

> Good: The summer had long since drawn to a close, and the verdant landscape had undergone an ominous transformation. Touched by the first October frosts, the forest glowed like a bed of tulips; and, all along the river bend, the painted

foliage, brightened by the autumnal sun, reflected its mingled colors upon the dark water below.

2. Introduce sentences occasionally with a participial phrase.

Poor: The boy was holding the injured puppy in his arms. He dashed quickly around the corner.

Good: Holding the injured puppy in his arms, the boy dashed quickly around the corner.

3. Invert the order of modifiers.

Normal: He stood there entranced.

Inverted: Entranced, he stood there.

4. Use a question occasionally.

Correct: The whole picture seemed different now. Something must have taken place.

Improved: The whole picture seemed different now. What could have taken place?

5. Use an infinitive phrase for introduction occasionally.

Correct: I should have looked at the book when I took it out.

Improved: To take out a book without looking at it was just like me.

6. Employ a bit of quotation once in a while.

Correct: He agreed that sea-sickness could be cured by one's remaining on land.

Improved: He agreed with Mark Twain, "A sure cure for sea-sickness is to lie on your back under a tree."

7. Use an adverbial clause for the subordinate idea.

Correct: I was frequently sent on errands. At times like these I took a book with me.

Improved: When I was sent on errands, I always took a book with me.

8. Introduce a sentence with a prepositional phrase.

Correct: I looked out the window. I could see the old man trudging up the street.

Improved: From my window I could see the old man trudging up the street.

9. Use a series of parallel constructions to gain suspense.

Poor: When the whistle blew, the spectators

straightened in their seats while the players took their positions. The game was beginning.

Good: The whistle blew; spectators straightened in their seats; the players took their positions; the game was on.

10. Throw in a figure of speech from time to time.

Examples: The storm swept the sky cleaner than a Dutch kitchen.

His words were ice-capped, splitting the air into tiny atoms.

Her thoughts leap-frogged at the idea.

And then, as we pointed out earlier in the book, let us not forget a cardinal principle: Read *constantly* and *carefully* the *best models*. Watch with ear as well as with eye how a thing is done by someone who knows how to do it. Read *widely* to discover how many different ways there are of writing effectively.

LET'S GO THE EXTRA MILE!

The difference between writing and good writing frequently hinges on the writer's preparation. Is he willing to be thorough? Anyone can do "skeleton" writing, but why not write to *sell*? That difference may easily lie with his attitude toward going the extra mile: *research, interview,* or *questionnaire.*

Not all fillers need them; few call for more than one. But the point is: If there is going to be any "meat" on the skeleton, you must set about collecting the data that will give strength to your writing.

The word *research* needs more than passing mention. One doesn't write an article simply by explaining facts without support for the statements made. You must be accurate in presenting details; you must not leave your reader with erroneous impressions. The writer's job is to *read* before he *writes*.

The method of note-taking, whether on three by five cards, scratch pad, or notebook paper, is of minor importance. The main thing is to provide yourself with *more* facts than you really need. It's an old rule of thumb— and a good one—to have on hand five times as much material as you need. To the beginner this much research probably sounds unnecessary, maintaining that if he isn't going to use all the notes he takes, why take them? He ignores two facts with such a theory: first, that if he's been thorough about taking notes, he already has a supply from which to draw for another article and second, the people that mail the checks for writing are experienced at judging a piece. They can readily detect whether the author had to squeeze hard to get a certain number of words he was aiming at, or whether by careful culling of the irrelevant notes, he has left an article that is meaty and appealing.

The *interview* is particularly valuable because it provides flavor to our writing and information difficult to secure in print. It should be considered only after three steps have been taken:

1. Acquaint yourself with all the facts you can gather about the person you're going to visit.

2. Make an appointment with that person before visiting him.

3. Have a very definite plan to follow when you get there. Often a list of questions submitted to him *in advance* of the visit will save time for both you and him at the time of the interview. But questions are not enough. Lead the person out; get him to talk freely. You'll soon be hearing anecdotes and sidelights that otherwise you'd never be able to include in your article.

The *questionnaire* is necessary, of course, when distance prevents an interview. It is the weaker medium but can still be effective in securing information if you plan it carefully. In so far as possible word the questions in such a way that the answers can be simple and short. Earlier we pointed out that the typed questionnaire should include sufficient space for the answers and that there should be space allowed at the end for general remarks. Be sure to enclose a stamped self-addressed envelope for the return of the information.

EXPECT TO REWRITE!

Like everyone else, you will find that as soon as you have finished one article, there will be a strong urge to get it into the mail. You want to speed it into print and to receive your check from the editor. Consequently, you will be overlooking the business of revision, a very important part of the trade of being a writer. In Chapter Four we mentioned letting an article "cool" before re-reading it, for without doubt your eyes and ears will pick up errors more readily after a lapse of time. But even more important, when you return to the manuscript, read it aloud, and often there will be many things you will want to change: word choice, construction, punctuation, perhaps a different viewpoint or shift of order.

Make up your mind that few articles are published without revision. And many of them have been revised and retyped several times. To neglect the practice is to hamper your chances of improvement, for only by constant effort to make the article the very best thing you can write can you speed your growth as a craftsman.

WORK FOR ACCURACY

Accuracy should apply to two phases of article writing:

1. As to *content*:

    (a) Are *all* the facts presented?

    (b) Are *names* included if the article calls for some? (And most of them do.)

    (c) Is the article too opinionated? (Only opinions based on cited facts will be accepted by readers. Be sure statements made are supported with carefully-sifted evidence.)

2. As to *mechanics*:

    (a) Is your grammar correct? Have you examined every sentence?

    (b) Is there agreement in number between subject and verb?

(c) Is there agreement between pronouns and their antecedents?

(d) Is the tense *sequence* correct?

(e) Have you made use of transitional devices? In other words, is the coherence of the whole article enhanced by a use of connecting words and phrases as you go from one paragraph to another?

(f) Has the title been planned to describe accurately the subject matter? Is it attractive? Is it concise?

ARRIVE EARLY!

Many magazines, you will discover, give top priority to articles in step with the calendar. Since one of their aims is to keep their publications as timely as possible, they are constantly making plans to anticipate the seasonal demands of their readers.

From five to eight months of a holiday, for instance, the editor is glad to see manuscripts coming in pertinent to the event. That means only one thing: that the writer begin early his campaign to place a seasonal article in a monthly magazine. If the manuscript is prepared early enough and submitted to an editor who rejects it, then the article must be sent out until sold. All of this takes time.

It perhaps will seem strange, almost impossible, to be doing articles on ice-skating when the August heat has you wilted. Personally I have found a little different scheme that works better for me. When, for instance, we are in the midst of the Christmas atmosphere, I can "think Christmas" better by writing an article or two right then. As I return to it for revision later, the problem of "mood" has been eliminated entirely.

Besides those on holidays, articles are frequently written on anniversaries of events, inventions, medical discoveries, erection of monuments, disasters. The historical importance of landmarks should not be overlooked, nor the dedication of state and national parks or birthplaces of famous statesmen.

Encyclopedias can supply background for many of these historical or biographical pieces. The essential requirement is a tie-in of the historical facts with an anniversary. Editors are alert to timeliness and they are especially pleased to have seasonal articles offered them.

When magazines use seasonal articles, they are likely to be found in the same issues each year. Study back issues, then, to see what subjects have appeal and how they were handled. It is not presumptuous, in fact, to tackle the same subject, but naturally the approach and treatment should be entirely different. Both should be *yours.*

HINTS THAT WILL HELP

1. Have a "catchy" beginning. I like to call it "Start by startling." If you have ever had any experience photographing a baby, you realize how important it is to get his attention focused on something and then in that moment of interest click the camera. We should be most painstaking with our opening paragraph to see that reader interest is aroused and focused.

Notice a few introductory paragraphs here and observe the approach made to the subject.

> One of the greatest mysteries of the universe lies some 4,000 miles directly under your feet. Ask any scientist about the earth's core and he will answer, "I don't know."

> Do you believe in fate? Or do you half-believe in a mythical Lady Luck who smiles on those whom she chooses? Nancy Windsor is not quite sure what she believes, either—except that life is full of surprises.

> So you want to write! You enjoyed your English classes, got good grades on themes, and your friends say you write exceptionally interesting letters. When they ask why you don't write for the magazines, you think it might be a good idea. You begin to dream.

2. Wherever possible, use the active voice. It gives sentences life, while passive voice is inclined to lull them to sleep.

> Passive: It *is* usually not *realized* how much planing and work *are being put* into such a project.
> Active: Not everybody *realizes* how much planning and work the committee *puts* into it.

3. Add a little humor when you can. Naturally there are many subjects that would not call for it. But, if appropriate, a little humorous quotation or a twist of phrasing can often furnish that added touch to one's writing.

Don't drag in something humorous for humor's sake. By all means, see that it is related to the subject.

4. End up with a bang! Though one of the most difficult phases of composition, the ending is still the most important. One must write *toward* the ending, for if it's going to be impressive, it must be delivered with a punch. It must also coincide in tone and content with that which has gone before.

Go over the list of details you are presenting. Decide which is the most forceful or perhaps unusual. Then leave that detail to the last. Your ending will decide what stays in the reader's mind.

CHAPTER FIVE

How to Sell What You Write

The writer of fillers and articles, like the writer of any other type of copy, must declare himself a salesman as well as a manufacturer. His course must be painstaking and logical. This portion of the book has been prepared with a view to helping the writer plan a strategy that will result in sales.

There is no substitute for good writing. But aside from an author's choice of words and their arrangement, there is no second factor more important than the editor's first impression of the manuscript. A department store clerk would be skeptical of making sales should the goods on her counter appear shoddy. Likewise, the writer whose manuscript is the only medium of contact with an editor should be extremely cautious about its arrangement, its accuracy, and its general appearance.

CORRECTLY PREPARE THE MANUSCRIPT

A glance at the busy executive's desk in today's publishing business should result in one conclusion: that certain accepted rules of manuscript preparation are compulsory. The instructions listed here are more than a matter of courtesy. They are the indispensable means of furthering your chances of a sale. Remembering, then, that your manuscript *is* your salesman and it represents *you,* by all means heed these requirements:

1. Use good quality paper eight and a half by eleven inches. Thin stock may cost slightly less to mail but it will not withstand travel. By the time a fuzzy-edged manuscript has had four rejections, what chance has the last editor to read it without bias?

2. Be sure that the manuscript is typed (not handwritten) neatly. If you can't type, hire a competent typist.

3. Keep the type face clean. Use a black ribbon.

4. Type your name and address, single spaced, in the upper left corner of the first page.

5. Record the length in the upper right corner of the first page. For example, 800 words. The mark of an amateur is to count as closely as 811 words. Always keep the figure in round numbers. Underneath that number write *Usual rates.*

6. Leave 1½ inch margins at both sides and type the title in capital letters at least one-third of the way down from the top. If you don't wish your real name used, under the title write "By .... (whatever pen name you use)."

7. All manuscripts must be double-spaced and on one side only.

8. Always make and keep carbon copies of manuscripts.

9. Number the pages (after the first one) in the upper right corner. In other words, start by writing the figure 2 on page 2. Do not place periods after numerals.

10. Be sure you are correct in spelling, punctuation, and capitalization.

11. Manuscripts of article length should be sent first

class. If not too bulky, they can be folded into thirds
and mailed in long envelopes. If, however, there is a
photograph accompanying the article, or if the manuscript
is bulky, mail it flat in a 9 by 12 envelope or fold it once
and place in a 6 by 9 envelope. Be sure to enclose a
stamped envelope of sufficient size to provide for its return in case the editor rejects it. It is a good idea to have
a supply of 6 by 9 and 6½ by 9½ envelopes; also 9 by 12
and 9½ by 12½ envelopes. In that way no size manuscript
and no size picture will go unaccommodated.

12. Carry out standard paragraph indentions
throughout the manuscript. The typists' rule of five
spaces is adequate.

13. Avoid stapling sheets together. The pages should
be loose but arranged in order when placed in envelopes.

14. Send your manuscript out with a businesslike
appearance. Besides the neat kraft envelope, use a business label carefully typed to the editor.

15. If you want words to appear in italics, under-
score them.

16. Keep your manuscripts neat and clean. If they
are returned to you spoiled and rumpled, retype the
pages that need it.

17. In most cases it is not necessary to enclose a
letter to the editor when submitting an article. (If you
have sold to other markets, it might be worth mentioning.
If the article represents a personal experience, you may
want to say so.) But bearing in mind that the editor is
a busy man, bother him as little as possible. If your
article is good, it will speak for itself anyway.

18. Though this book deals with articles and fillers
only, the question of book-length material often arises.
Book-length manuscripts, especially those exceeding two

hundred typed pages, until a few years ago were sent by express, prepaid, and the publishers were instructed to return unacceptable ones the same way, with shipping charges collect. This method can still be used, but there is a less costly one that has proved just as effective. It applies, however, only to parcels weighing one pound or more. Mark the package "Educational Materials." You will pay, without regard to zone, a low cost of something like nine cents for the first pound and five cents for each additional pound or fraction. If photographs or other illustrations are to be included in the manuscript, they, too, can become part of the package. These parcels should be insured at regular parcel post rates.

By enclosing a return envelope marked "Educational Materials" and with your return address and stamps, you can be assured of the same service at a later date, should the publisher find your book unsuitable for his needs.

You may choose to enclose a letter of instructions to the editor concerning shipment. In that case, simply indicate on the outside of the package: "Letter enclosed," and the letter postage will be added to your total postage fee. The accompanying letter can, of course, be attached to the outside of the package.

Book manuscripts and other bulky manuscripts are best shipped in a box such as typewriter paper comes in.

19. In book manuscripts, begin all chapters and major divisions on a new page, omitting periods after headings and subheadings. Whatever style or method you adopt at the beginning of your manuscript, follow through consistently to the end.

STUDY THE MARKETS

We have pointed out earlier that there is no more important an investment than the time used in studying the markets for the particular field of your choice. The chief purpose is to prepare you for selling your articles. The best article in the world won't sell if it is sent to the wrong markets. Before submitting a manuscript to a particular editor, secure several issues of his magazine and read them from cover to cover. In that way, you will save time for both him and yourself by not submitting an article of length and type entirely unsuited to his use.

Study market lists, too (discussed later in this chapter), not just to find addresses to which to send your fillers and articles, but to learn the over-all requirements of the many different publications. This kind of study will gradually develop a market sense.

It is important also that you realize that magazines change in editorial policy and are continuing to change. Never be foolish enough to use an old magazine as a guide to current trends, even though the contents especially delight you. Sample every magazine you think might buy your work. With just a little study of what those editors are publishing, you can soon detect the magazine's policy, its apparent needs, its style, and at the same time can save yourself headaches and postage.

As we pointed out in Chapter Four, the article must reach the editor so that he can use it while it is timely. Newspaper features are often prepared from four to six weeks ahead of publication. Magazine editors generally select their material five to six months—sometimes even more—in advance. Because an article may not sell the first time it is submitted, it should be sent out early enough to allow for two or three other editors before it passes the time limit.

The article not associated with a holiday or special event or a particular time of year can remain in circulation until it does sell.

SLANT YOUR MATERIAL

At least unconsciously every writer slants. He has something to say; he feels compelled to say it; and furthermore, he is unconsciously addressing someone or something. Yet actually we should never slant at magazines. We should slant at readers—at kinds of people.

The writer must be consistent. He must keep the type of reader audience in minds as he writes. Obviously if you have prepared a clever little how-to filler on a new kind of kite, you'll not send it to an adult publication. And neither will the tone of the piece be mature and sophisticated. If perhaps the subject selected would appeal to both levels, you should write both separately and with distinctly different approaches, thereby earning twice as much.

An important factor in slanting, other than subject and tone, is wordage. Most of the market lists appearing in the various writers' magazines include wordage desired by the editors. If the magazine specializes in 2,000-worders with illustrations, send nothing as a substitute. It all goes back to studying the market.

STEPPING STONES TO SALES

A cardinal sin in this business of writing is the failure to attack it in an orderly, almost scientific manner. Wasted motion, time, and talent are the fruits of anything less than logical procedure.

1. Select the subject. Make sure it is not so broad a topic that your article will have no definite impact on its readers.

2. Check the *Reader's Guide to Periodical Literature* in your local library. If your subject has been recently and completely covered, drop it, unless you are sure you can come up with an entirely new, fresh approach.

3. Explore the markets for your article idea. To what type of reader will the subject appeal? Who publishes magazines for that type of reader? Believe me, you can't judge an article theme fairly unless you have a market concept.

4. Once you are convinced the subject is a good one, do a sufficient amount of research on it to guarantee a satisfying article. Include anecdotes to give it life. Don't be alarmed if you gather so much material you'd be better off developing two articles.

5. Make sure that the article theme is within your capabilities and experience. Don't sell yourself short, by any means, but there is nothing more ruinous to one's morale than to find that you've tackled something too big to handle. Far better that you aim at a humble market with a simple article you can't resist writing! The lesser-known magazines are often the best markets for the beginners; the editors have fewer articles from which to select. The pay may not be so gratifying, but the maga-

zines are easier to sell to and it's more practical to make two or three sales than to strive for one big one that doesn't come through. Besides, if you work constantly to better your own record, you will soon write yourself out of the smaller markets.

SHOULD ONE QUERY AN EDITOR FIRST?

There is a wide difference of opinion regarding queries. For the beginning writer? Definitely not. An article of 500, 1,000, 1,500 words or even more—written well, and steered toward a likely market—needs no preliminary query. Send the article instead.

For the more experienced writer who feels he has graduated from humble publications, the emphasis on querying is somewhat more pronounced. Some editors prefer a letter stating two or three article ideas at one time. If the writer has only the theme idea of an article, not the completed article, and has made an outline of it or has written a description of the proposed piece, he may be saving himself (and the editor) a lot of time. He may discover any number of things: that the editor just doesn't like the subject matter, or that the editor has a huge stock of purchased articles ahead and can take no more at present, or that he has previously purchased an article on a similar subject.

If you are an authority in a particular field or have had actual experience that prompted the piece, very likely you can interest a magazine editor in your idea. However, he has reason to be concerned if you simply list a half-dozen subject possibilities of diverse range and ask him about your chances of having one accepted.

And again, in case you grow from an article writer

to a book author, you'll find that the procedure for selling a book of nonfiction is somewhat different. After you have consulted a writers' market guide and made a list of potential publishers, organize a good query letter that can be used as many times as you need. Don't make it detailed and involved. Tell the editor what you have to offer and how you have handled it, how long the finished manuscript is—in words, not pages. Tell him what else, if anything, will accompany the manuscript. Then on a separate sheet include a well-prepared outline of its contents. Always keep a carbon copy of everything you submit.

It is permissible to send several query letters out at the same time, but avoid sending any sample material to more than one publisher at a time, and only then when it is requested. Publishers, when interested in the information presented in your query or impressed with the outline you have submitted, will undoubtedly ask to see at least two or three chapters.

TO WHOM DO YOU ADDRESS A QUERY LETTER?

To the same editor who will eventually read your article if you get the green light. If the magazine has department editors, send it to the one who specializes in what you're writing. If you are in doubt, send it to the editor-in-chief or the managing editor. By all means, use their *names*, not their positions. You can find their exact names and offices on the table of contents page of one of their recent issues. Their names are usually given also in the various market guides.

WHAT ABOUT AN AGENT?

For the inexperienced writer, contacting an agent would be folly. In fact, one shoud keep in mind that there are several types of writing that an agent is unwilling to handle: material slanted toward juveniles; poetry; fillers; short articles by unknowns—to mention a few.

Many authors with years of experience have never used an agent. Prolific novelists and writers of book length non-fiction, on the other hand, depend entirely upon their agents to take care of the irksome and time-consuming details of author-publisher contact.

There is really no one quite so close to the manuscript as the one who prepared it. And if you have confidence in that piece, your enthusiasm and "sales force" are usually adequate for convincing the editor.

WHAT ABOUT ILLUSTRATIONS?

Naturally with such fillers as jokes, anecdotes, epigrams, quizzes, letters, recipes, etc., the question of illustrations never arises. But often with fillers of other types and articles running from 600 to 1,000 or more words, we must choose for ourselves the wisest course. The point should be obvious to every writer. If it is a type that is widely appealing, it needs a first-rate illustration appropriate to it. Many writers experience rejection of their work because the pictures were either missing or inadequate.

Some magazines do not use illustrations. Some use only pen-and-ink sketches or other drawings by their own staff artists. Therefore you can see the need for understanding markets before submitting manuscripts. Nearly all editors pay additionally for the photographs used; a few include them when paying for the article.

To include illustrations does not always mean that the writer must take the pictures himself. If you *can* do a reasonably good job with your camera, more power to your purse, but it is frequently done in other ways. Perhaps you interview a businessman. Together you decide to write an article on his recently renovated store. In most cases the merchant himself will offer to take care of that expense for he's probably been wanting a picture for his own use anyhow. The how-to article, if centered around someone other than the author, can likewise be accompanied by a photograph furnished by the one involved.

Local newspapers which carry photos and from which you glean a rewrite possibility are very obliging in lending material that has already been used. Often it is advisable to contact advertising agencies or public relations bureaus to secure pictures. For example, suppose you write a little 800-word article on the quaint old Gaspé Peninsula. It seems suitable for a teen-agers' magazine, but the editor demands one gloss print. It will cost you nothing but time and postage to secure some illustrative material from Canadian National Railways.

Always seek excellence of illustration. Remember that you are competing with the other fellow who may have at his elbow splendid pictures. The size of photos is also important; usually eight by ten and five by seven are the most desirable.

Charts, diagrams, maps, blueprints, and working plans are all legitimate substitutes for photographs and are preferred by the editors of some magazines. All we can say is study the magazine you have in mind and settle for yourself the proper choice. In other words, the job of slanting is not finished until the idea, the type of article, and picture-or-not issue are all settled in the writer's mind!

WHAT SHOULD THE ARTICLE
WRITER'S LIBRARY CONTAIN?

Just as the doctor's office contains a ready-reference and many other supplies, so the writer should have certain tools available for his use as he conducts this business of writing. Here is a list of what I call the basic few, but as time goes on and the writer shows progress, he will undoubtedly add many others of his own choice.

1. *The Holy Bible.* No more beautiful literature can be found than that in the world's "best seller." Its graceful phrasing, its rhythm, its figures of speech, its beautiful simplicity, its truth—all these can serve as inspiration for the writer.

2. *A good dictionary.*

3. *Roget's Thesaurus of English Words and Phrases.*

4. *A handbook of English.* One should by all means guard against inaccuracies in English usage. Editors tell us that no phase of the mechanics of writing so irks them to the point of rejecting manuscripts as faulty punctuation and capitalization. Even a small paperbook reference similar to that used by office secretaries is better than nothing. Sometimes, unfortunately, it is more than simple mechanics. It is faulty grammar that is inexcusable.

5. *A good market guide.* No one can possibly be successful in placing his manuscripts if he has no knowledge of current trends and demands being made by the

many book and magazine editors. Besides the market lists appearing frequently in various writers' magazines, there are several fine books available, one of which should be on every writer's desk. For example: *Writer's Market*, edited by Kirk Polking, Writer's Digest, Cincinnati, Ohio, 54210, priced $7.95; *The Writer's Handbook*, edited by A. S. Burack, The Writer, 8 Arlington Street, Boston, Mass.; Literary Market Place, edited by Anne J. Richter, R. R. Bowker Company, 1180 Avenue of the Americas, New York, N. Y., 10036, priced $7.45.

6. *Free Bulletin and Price List of pamphlets issued by the United States Government.* For a nominal sum the writer of articles can find an inexhaustible source of material from which to draw. By writing to Supt. of Documents, Washington, D. C., you can secure the free bulletin listing these hundreds of booklets and the small fee for each.

7. *A weekly newspaper.*

8. *A good writers' magazine.* The beginning writer will find a good writers' magazine especially helpful, for they often provide the inspiration, advice, or encouragement that he is seeking. In addition, from time to time the market lists he finds published there will apply to the filler and article needs of the moment. For example: *Writer's Digest*, Cincinnati, Ohio, 54210; *Author and Journalist*, Suite 1028, National Press Building, Washington, D. C., 20004; *The Writer*, 8 Arlington Street, Boston, Mass. 02116.

DO'S FOR WRITERS

1. Be a good bookkeeper. Keep a record of where your manuscripts go, when submitted, when returned,

how many words each, and amount each sold for. The trick in marketing a filler once it is written is to eliminate hit-and-miss submission by setting up a series of buyers' lists. For each filler written you should have a separate notebook page or a 4x6 card on which is the first entry as mentioned *plus* a list of all other possible markets for that particular filler. You are not displaying pessimism toward the sale of that article; it is merely a time-saving device. If the piece is rejected by No. 1, all you have to do is to consult the card, place the filler in a clean envelope, and fire it on to No. 2. Naturally you will submit to the highest paying markets first, provided the article has been properly slanted.

2. If you're going to be successful at this business, you *must* keep a lot of fillers in the mail.

3. Just because fillers are short, your tendency may be to single space them on small pieces of paper. Don't do it! Use the standard eight and a half by eleven bond and double space. The best plan is to prepare no fewer than five jokes, three anecdotes, five epigrams, eight household hints, etc. on separate sheets when submitting to an editor. It is a postage-saving device and it also improves your chances for having one or two of each submission accepted by the editor. In longer articles such a plan would be ridiculous.

4. Organize a filing system. The selling writer is the one who is systematic about his research. So true is this that a clipping file is a *must*. Nine by twelve envelopes or letter-size file folders will work very well. As mentioned in another chapter, label them to indicate type: Anecdotes, Recipes, etc. Frequent study of the file and a persistent revision of it, as well as adding to it while

ideas are fresh in your mind, are necessary if your system is to be really workable.

5. Use the simplest language that your subject will afford. The simplest writing is the best writing because it has the widest appeal.

6. Have a daily program and stick to it.

DONT'S FOR WRITERS

1. Don't submit several copies of the same manuscript to different editors. The practice is unethical and can cause embarrassing situations.

2. Don't "dress up" a manuscript. Stick to the rules presented earlier in this chapter.

3. Don't get discouraged when rejection slips come back. By keeping plenty of material on editors' desks, make the rejection slip serve as a challenge or test of endurance. If you'll do that, you can't help selling before long.

4. Don't be afraid to rewrite. Someone has aptly said, "You have not learned to write until you have learned to rewrite." Be critical of your own work, admit weaknesses you see in it when compared with published material, and revise carefully. Don't be satisfied with anything short of the best.